IT MIGHT HAVE BEEN RAINING

*To Steve
with best wishes*

Robert Greenham

IT MIGHT HAVE BEEN RAINING

The Remarkable Story of
J. M. Barrie's Housekeeper
at Black Lake Cottage

Robert Greenham

WITH A FOREWORD BY ANDREW BIRKIN

Elijah Editions

Published June 2005 by
Elijah Editions
Gunning House
60 Upper Fant Road
Maidstone, Kent ME16 8DN
elijah@fierychariot.co.uk
www.fierychariot.co.uk
01622 750943

© Robert Greenham 2005
© Foreword, Andrew Birkin 2005

The Author asserts the moral right to
be identified as the author of this work

Printed and bound in Great Britain by
Kall Kwik, 72 Bank Street, Maidstone, Kent ME14 1SN
print@maidstone.kallkwik.co.uk
01622 688966

All rights reserved.
No part of this book may be reproduced,
transmitted or stored in an information retrieval system
in any form or by any means,
graphic, electronic or mechanical,
including photocopying, taping and recording,
without prior written permission from the publisher.

A CIP catalogue record for this book is available
from the British Library

ISBN 0-9550502-0-0

To the memory of my mother
Marian Llewelyn Greenham (née Jones), 1911-1991

A safe but sometimes chilly way of recalling the past is to force open a crammed drawer. If you are searching for anything in particular you don't find it, but something falls out at the back that is often more interesting.

From *Peter Pan, To the Five – A Dedication*
by J. M. Barrie, 1860-1937

Contents

Illustrations

Foreword by Andrew Birkin

Introduction and Acknowledgements   1

Prologue   11

Chapter 1	13
Chapter 2	20
Chapter 3	31
Chapter 4	40
Chapter 5	49
Chapter 6	65
Chapter 7	69
Chapter 8	77
Chapter 9	80

Epilogue   85

Appendix   89

Sources and Selective bibliography   99

Index   101

Illustrations

Front and back cover

Mabel and Fred in the garden at The Boynes, Medstead, July 1904 (Photo-postcard in author's collection)

Inside front and back cover

Postcard (enlarged) from Fred to Mabel, August 1904 (Photo-postcard in author's collection)

Between pages 64 and 65

Mabel Bessie Llewellyn, about 1903 (Author's collection)

Mary Ansell in 1891 (From an engraving by 'MK')

Mary Ansell, about 1894 (By permission of Andrew Birkin)

J. M. Barrie in about 1903 (Photograph by G. C. Beresford)

J. M. Barrie with Luath at Leinster Corner, Kensington, in 1904 (By permission of Andrew Birkin)

Alice Kinge (née Lamport) and her second daughter, Myrtle Joyce Kinge, 1906 (By permission of Pat Pullinger)

Archibald Ellis Jones and Mabel, Wrexham, 1915 (Author's collection)

Mabel with Robert Greenham and Billy, in the garden at Merryweather, Ditton, 1947 (Author's collection)

Foreword

Robert Greenham's little portrait of his grandmother Mabel Llewellyn is more than just a delightful ramble below Edwardian stairs, for it throws new light on her employers – J. M. Barrie and his unhappy wife Mary. Mabel became the Barries' housekeeper at Black Lake Cottage in the spring of 1903 – two years after that terrible summer of 1901, in which the Davies boys had acted out *The Boy Castaways* to Barrie's camera. But if she'd missed the prelude to *Peter Pan*, she had arrived just in time for the main act, for it was during her watch that Barrie finally penned 'that terrible masterpiece'.

In Barriesque mode, Robert has chosen to act as his grandmother's amanuensis, allowing her to tell her story in her own words, albeit through the medium of her grandson. This has led him to undertake a good deal of research, which has in turn unearthed a number of hitherto unknown facts, as well as plausible speculations, with respect to Barrie and his creations, not least the possible origin of that nefarious pirate, Captain Hook.

But it is Mabel Llewellyn herself who here takes centre stage, and rightly so since this is her story, not Barrie's. Her great good fortune was to have had so celebrated – and generous – an employer ... as well as an equally generous (albeit less famous) grandson as her fanciful biographer. I hope her story will bring as much pleasure to others as it has to me.

Andrew Birkin
Wales, May 2005

Introduction

Tell me something: What do you do when your boiler fails in deep midwinter, leaving you with no heating and no hot water? You phone for expert help, that's what. After all, you've got a contract for maintenance and emergency callouts. But the help won't come for three days, so you'll need to do something soon or else your house will get very cold.

You switch on the gas fire in the sitting room, and then you nip out in your car to the electrical store in town, a couple of miles away, buy two or three ten-quid heaters, bring them back, plug them in and switch them on. That's the heating sorted. Then you switch on the kettle and make a quick cup of tea or instant coffee to help you warm up. When it gets dark, you switch on your lights, and, come dinner time, you switch on the oven, or the grill, or the hob, or the microwave oven, or any combination of them. Or maybe you'll simply order a take-away meal by phone for delivery thirty minutes later. Hot water for washing up afterwards? No problem, just boil a couple of kettles of water.

When it's bedtime you might fancy a bath. Aha! Not a chance, not unless you have an immersion heater. A wash, then? OK, but you may need to boil a few more kettles of water, and carry them upstairs to the bathroom. And it'll be the same again in the morning.

It's a bit of a pain, this, isn't it? And it wastes time. But you can manage. Manage, that is, until the electricity supply goes off, which it has just done. So what do you do now? Ah, yes. Of course. You use the gas. Er, no. Sorry, but that's just gone off, too. You wouldn't believe it, would you? A digger working down the road has just severed the mains.

So, now you've got no heating, no cooking, no lighting and no hot water. And the house is going to get cold. What will you do now? Light a fire? Sorry, but you installed the gas fire in the only open fireplace in your modern, super-efficient house. Go out and buy a Calor gas cylinder and stove? OK, but how many? Anyway, it's now Saturday evening and the shops will have closed. You may have to wait until Monday. And haven't you forgotten something else? Your fridge and freezer have started to defrost. Still, look on the bright side: once the house gets cold that won't be such a big problem, will it? Just think: this could have happened during a heatwave, then you'd have been in trouble, what with all that food thawing out. Oops. Sorry. Just trying to be funny.

Up to date with the washing, are you? It's not much fun doing it with only cold water, that's for sure. And in the sink. By hand. The machine won't work, nor will the dryer, nor the iron. But you need some clean underwear? And you'll give it a go? Excellent. That's the spirit. Hang on, I'll give you a hand. Hey, guess what? Yes, that's right, the water supply seems to have dried up. Look at this: I turn on the tap but no water comes out. That's funny. It's never done that before, has it?

D'you know, I'm beginning to think you might be in a spot of bother here. In fact, I definitely think things are starting to look really serious, don't you?

Oh yes, I almost forgot. There's a funny smell out the front. It's not very nice. I bet you've forgotten about that suspected blocked sewer under the front lawn. That man still hasn't been to clear it, has he? Well, I understand. You've had other problems to worry about lately, haven't you? But this could become a health hazard, so maybe you you'd better phone him again.

What's that? Don't tell me the phone line's dead. Oh, I say, that is rotten luck. Well, there's always your mobile. Call him on that. What? It was stolen in the pub at lunchtime? What's the world coming to? I tell you what, then: drive over to his place and have a word with him. With a bit of luck, he won't have gone out. I'll hold the fort while you're gone.

Hello, that was quick. You were gone only five minutes. What do you mean, you haven't left yet? The car won't start? Oh dear, this really isn't your day, is it? You know, I always said you never should have eaten your carrier pigeon. All right, all right! Keep your hair on! I'm sorry, but I was only joking. I find it helps to keep a sense of humour at times like this. They'll probably sack that digger driver, but that won't help you one bit, I'm afraid. How many of you are there in the house, anyway? Just you? Oh, well, that's not too bad. Things could be worse. They could be a lot worse. You could have had a houseful of guests coming tomorrow and staying for a week or two, and maybe some more coming each day for lunch and dinner - say about twenty each day - then what would you have done?

I'll tell you what you would have done: you would have walked a mile in my grandmother's shoes.

I invented this scenario to help set the scene of my grandmother's home and workplace just over a hundred years ago. Picture a house in the country, in 1903, just two miles from the nearest town. There's no electricity, no gas, no mains water and no main sewer. There's no central heating, no double glazing, no loft insulation and no cavity wall insulation. There's no switchable lighting. In the kitchen there's no grill, no microwave oven, no fridge, no freezer, no automatic washing machine, no tumble drier, no dishwasher, no food processor ...

Elsewhere in the house, there's no vacuum cleaner, no floor polisher, no hair dryer, no heated rollers, curlers or straighteners, and no electric shavers. There's no telephone, no radio, no television, no computer. There are no do-it-yourself power tools. And outside, there's no car.

So what is there, then?

There's a lot of hard work, and it all takes a considerable amount of time. Inventions, technological advances, labour-saving devices ... How easily such terms roll of the tongue, but can you imagine what life was like only a hundred years ago? Can you? It's not easy, and here's why:

Starting with the present year, 2005, let's turn the clock back a bit. Let's go back just ten years. How different were things in the home then? Did we have the same things as we do now? Pretty well. Hardly anyone had mobile phones, though. OK, go back another ten years. Still not much different. Not many computers, though. Back another ten? OK, the home computers have gone.

And another ten? That's the electronic calculators and most of the microwave ovens gone. Go back another ten, to 1955, halfway back to our target year. Still not a lot of difference, certainly not if you can afford the latest household equipment and gadgets, although most homes do not have central heating now.

It's no wonder we take so much for granted when, from year to year, and even from decade to decade, we, in the western world see so little real change in our domestic lives nowadays. Yet, jump back the other fifty-odd years, to the spring of 1903, and we find that only the wealthy own an automobile, with the British national speed limit about to be raised from fourteen to twenty miles per hour. In America we find man trying to achieve sustained powered flight in a contraption called a heavier-than-air flying machine; by the end of the year he'll manage to rise a few feet off the ground and fly about a sixth of a mile – at a speed which wouldn't have broken the British highways speed limit of the time. Who, apart from the likes of H. G. Wells, could have predicted supersonic jet-powered flight within forty-five years, or that within seventy years man would visit the moon? And while supply networks of electricity, gas, water and telephony were being developed in the towns and cities of Britain in 1903, it would be several more years before rural communities would be so served.

Right. Back to my grandmother at the country house. Here she is, twenty-four years of age and not long arrived to start her first job as a housekeeper. In a few days, the owner and his wife will be coming down from London to stay for a long weekend. They'll be bringing some guests with them. A few weeks later, they'll be back with six more guests, and staying for a week or two. They are famous, wealthy people who are used to, and expect, high standards in everything. And there will be another twelve or more guests of similar standing visiting each daytime and evening. So, let's see: that'll be eight seated together for breakfast, and twenty or more for lunch and dinner, every day. All food and drink must be fresh, or freshly prepared. And that's just the catering. Let's take a look at some of the other tasks:

there will be rather a lot of clearing-up, sweeping, scrubbing, dusting, cleaning and polishing; washing-up and drying; washing, rinsing, mangling, drying and ironing, or spongeing and pressing. There are lots of lamps to be serviced. In the mornings, cups of tea must be served to the residents in their rooms, and hot water will be needed in each bedroom as well as the bathroom. If it turns chilly, fires will need to be lit and maintained, and almost every room has a fireplace. Nobody should be kept waiting for anything. Good records must be kept, for everything has to be properly accounted for. How is she going to cope?

We'll make it easier for her: we'll provide oil for the lamps, ample supplies of coal and logs for the fires and kitchen range, and we'll put a spring in the garden which, hopefully, will not run dry. How's that? Oh yes, and we'll give her an experienced housemaid to start with, and a bit more help when the guests arrive.

This is the story of what happened to a young woman when, for the first time in her life, she answered an advertisement for a housekeeper and, halfway through the interview with the advertiser, a Mr Winter, discovered that the other man present was none other than the writer and dramatist J. M. Barrie, and that it was he, and not the advertiser, who required the services of a housekeeper.

Mabel Bessie Llewellyn was born on January 27th, 1879, at 118 High Street, Poole, Dorset, a daughter of a tea merchant and grocer. She was the fourth of nine children: three boys, three girls, then three more boys. The seventh baby died after just eight days but the remainder enjoyed mainly long and healthy lives.

In April 1910 Mabel married postman Archibald Ellis Jones, a widower with four children, in Wrexham in North Wales. Mabel and Archie had two children, Marian Llewelyn Jones, my mother, and James Llewelyn Jones. A few months after war broke out, Archie joined the army and was immediately posted to Egypt, leaving Mabel with all the children. They planned to emigrate to Canada after the war but Archie never returned; he was transferred to Salonika, in Greece, where he died from adbominal shrapnel injuries sustained when a bomb fell on the town in July 1917.

In 1923 Mabel married again, to Arthur George Hann in Nether Compton, Dorset, but the marriage failed within two years, and Arthur died two years later, in 1927. Thereafter Mabel remained a widow until her death on May 26th, 1967, at the home of her daughter in East Malling, Kent.

Mabel was my grandmother.

As she was the eldest girl in the family, Mabel's schooling was cut short by the need for her to stay at home to help bring up her four younger siblings. Finally, when she could be spared, she trained for a commission in the Salvation Army. Within little more than two years of becoming a Captain, however, she turned to domestic service for a living. Between periods of child rearing and caring for members of family, most of which meant returning to her beloved Dorset, Mabel worked in several counties as a housekeeper. Among her employers were J. M. Barrie, Barrie's sister Maggie Winter, William Thomas, Brigadier-General Vaughan, Gwendolen Thomas and the English amateur champion golfer Miss Jeanne Bisgood, CBE.

Mabel's most memorable experience as a housekeeper was when she worked for J. M. Barrie (not then knighted) and his wife, Mary, at their rural summer home: Black Lake Cottage, near Farnham in Surrey. Mabel lived and worked there continuously during most of 1903, and then intermittently for a few years more.

James Matthew Barrie was born on May 9th 1860 at Kirriemuir, Scotland, the ninth of ten children of hand-loom weaver David Barrie and his wife Margaret Ogilvy. The fourth and fifth children had died in infancy. Barrie was educated at Dumfries Academy and Edinburgh University. Aiming to become an author, he started earning a living as a leader-writer on the Nottingham Journal. He held the job for about two years before returning briefly to Kirriemuir, from where he started sending unsolicited articles to various publications based in

London. On the strength of some success with articles published in the St James's Gazette in 1884, Barrie moved to London, and by 1887 he was contributing articles to many of the country's leading publications. In 1888 he wrote his first novel, and thereafter many novels and plays. Barrie married the actress Mary Ansell on July 9th 1894. They had no children, however, and were divorced in 1909. Barrie was knighted in 1913 and he became Rector of St Andrews University in the same year. He died in London on June 19th 1937 and was buried at Kirriemuir with his parents and some of his siblings.

Barrie's most remembered work is his play, *Peter Pan*, which opened at the Duke of York's Theatre, London, on December 27th 1904. It was the announcements, during 2004, of a number of events to mark the centenary of *Peter Pan* which prompted me to research and write my grandmother's story.

Mabel Llewellyn did not keep a diary, nor did she write down anything of her experiences. Fortunately, however, in 1953 she consented to the writing of an article about part of her time with Barrie. The article was written by one of her former employers, Gwendolen Thomas, and was published in John O'London's Weekly. That article, and my recollections of Mabel talking about her life experiences, gave me my starting point.

While drawing on descriptions of people, places and events found within biographies of Barrie, and in other published writings, the identities and lives of the domestic staff in Barrie's and other related households during those early years of the twentieth century have had to be uncovered, with varying degrees of success, through research elsewhere. Some of the sources were not available to Barrie's biographers of the mid and late twentieth century - the British Censuses of 1881, 1891 and 1901, for example - and the ability to track down present-day relations and descendants of some of my grandmother's contemporaries has been made easier through the wonder of the world wide web. Of the employees mentioned in my book, only Barrie's chauffeur of the time, Frederick, has proved impossible to identify. Consequently, and regretfully, I could not search for any descendants or other relatives of his. Should any such persons happen to read this little book I would be most interested to hear from them.

This is essentially a true story. I have attempted to step into Mabel's shoes of a hundred years ago, and to think like she would have thought, both at that time and later when looking back on that part of her life. I have traced her journeys and visited her homes and workplaces. While I have added a little imagination to my knowledge and the results of my research, I have not knowingly distorted any facts. I believe the result is a realistic account embracing real people, real places and real events, all set in time and described as accurately as possible so as to be true to their memory. Recognising that my book may be studied by historians and researchers, I have included an Afterword which comprises additional factual information and an explanation of where I used my imagination to fill in some gaps in my knowledge.

As part of my research I joined ANON, the J. M. Barrie Society. On its lively online forum, one of its members responded to one of my fanciful suggestions concerning the origin of the name of *Peter Pan*'s character, Captain James Hook, with something approaching a diatribe which began: "Who in the name of ******** **** gives a **** *** **** who Hook was, or is, or might have been? He exists on the written page; and sometimes if we are very lucky, perhaps, on a good night, he exists on stage. Why are you analyzing the poor villain, and everyone else in that priceless fantasy to a point where the magic disappears? What charmed you as a child is still there. Why make an English lesson of it? We need the magic! We need a Neverland. And Neverland quickly disappears when reality gets in the way." This was a good point well made. I am grateful to that member for reminding me of the need to retain a healthy balance between reality and imagination, and to keep a sense of proportion. I hope I have achieved this despite persisting with a few thoughts and suggestions based upon my research. If these provoke a little discussion among Barriephiles, and others, that is all to the good.

Some readers of my book may find themselves wanting to

learn more about J. M. Barrie. I hope so, for I have presented merely a glimpse of the author at the height of his literary success, and have indicated only a little of the tragedy, both in the life and of the life, of this complex man. In telling my grandmother's story, I have indicated that there was a great deal more to Barrie than *Peter Pan*. As it is, I have deliberately refrained from attempting to explain how *Peter Pan* came into being, and how Barrie reworked his famous play, for that has been done many times - as has the story of how and why Barrie befriended first the Davies boys, then their mother, then their father, and the nature and development of his relationships with them. Such explanations are, of course, a prerequisite of any complete biography of Barrie.

At the time of writing this introduction, a new biography by Lisa Chaney waits in the wings. Whatever merits it may possess, I unhesitatingly recommend reading Andrew Birkin's authoritative and lavishly illustrated biography *J. M. Barrie and the Lost Boys* which was one of my main published sources of information.

If a reader's only prior encounter with J. M. Barrie has been the recent film *Finding Neverland*, then a viewing of *J. M. Barrie and the Lost Boys*, now available on DVD, will provide a more accurate account of the middle portion of Barrie's life. This is a 4½ hour television drama written by Andrew Birkin and produced by the BBC in 1978 under the title of *The Lost Boys*, with Ian Holm providing the definitive Barrie. It should be realised, however, that this resource is no substitute for the book bearing the same title; each complements the other and is essential to gaining a full understanding of Barrie and his world.

The internet is a source of much information and detail. As always, the researcher should beware inaccuracies. These two sites, both of which include forums, should satisfy most needs:

Andrew Birkin's site, jmbarrie: www.jmbarrie.co.uk
ANON: The J. M. Barrie Society: www.jmbarrie.net

Those whose chief interests are centred around Peter Pan should see also:

c20th Peter Pan: www.c20th.com/peterpan.htm
Peter Pan Fan.com: www.peterpanfan.com/new/home.php

I gratefully acknowledge the help and encouragement given to me in various ways by the following people: John Archer, Jennifer Barnett, Andrew Birkin, Keith Brown, Kevin Brown, John Clayton, Graham Collyer, Olivia Cotton, Laura Duguid, Mark Elvers, John Franklin, Joe Gramm, Rachel Greenham, Chris Hellier of Farnham Museum, Sue Hesse, Dixie Jenks, Susan Jermyn, Rose Kempshall, Stella Monaghan Addy, Simon Moss, Margie O'Brien, Pat Pullinger, Samantha Reynolds, Melodye Benson Rosales, David Skipper, Pamela Jane Smith, Karen Thompson of the Salvation Army Heritage Centre, Steve Walters, Ursula Whitaker, Peter Wynne Willson. Special mention deservedly goes to Andrew Birkin for responding to my questions with patience, tolerance and understanding. I thank him for advising and guiding me with his expertise and his renowned knowledge of J. M. Barrie and the Davies family, and for generously offering to write a Foreword before I dared to ask that last favour of him.

Robert Greenham
Maidstone, May 2005

Prologue

But wider over many heads
The starry voice ascending spreads,
Awakening, as it waxes thin,
The best in us to him akin;
And every face to watch him raised,
Puts on the light of children praised;

From *The Lark Ascending* by George Meredith, 1828-1909

Everyone has secrets. When I died I took mine with me. With lingering thoughts of my loved ones and fading memories of my long, satisfying life of service to others, I happily cast off the tether of life. Wrapped in the warmth of love, all pain gone, I drifted gently up and away, peaceful and contented and sure of my destiny, along the way soaring high above the rolling landscapes of my life and my beloved Dorset. Some weeks later, in accordance with my wishes, my ashes were scattered in the summer breeze on Ballard Down, just over Old Harry's chalky shoulder, where cows graze on buttercups, clover and daisies, and skylarks rise and warble and trill all day, and from where the views of the Isle of Purbeck, Poole Harbour, the coastline and the sea, right across to the Isle of Wight, are glorious and uplifting. I always believed I could fly, for gravity exerts no pull on the spirit. My death was so easy, unlike my life.

Unlike my life in my twenties, for example, when, as a new housekeeper to J. M. Barrie, I was a happy young woman, still single, and with not the slightest inkling of the tragedy which the Great War would bring to my life, and to the lives of my two dear young children and four step-children, fourteen years later. Those early exciting, demanding, sometimes carefree times I recall now, a hundred years later, through my grandson and his research, and just a little imagination.

"Robert, can you hear me?"

"Granny! Is that you? Where are you? I can't see you."

"I'm here, within you, where I've always been, and where I'll always be. You're a part of me, don't forget. Now listen, my boy. Do you remember what I told you about my life as a young woman?"

"Yes."

"And my time at Black Lake Cottage?"

"I certainly do."

"Good. I'd like you to write it down properly because I never got around to it, and I never kept a diary. I want my descendants to know something of my life and times. Will you do this for me, please?"

"Granny, I'd love to. Thank you for asking me."

"Don't forget the bit about the rabbits, or the old hat box, or James Hook."

"No, of course not. But what about the people?"

"The Barries? What's left to tell? Hasn't it all been said?"

"Maybe. There have been several biographies but some of their writers either didn't know James Barrie personally, or didn't meet him until years after your time working for him, or were not even born during his lifetime, and they rightly focused on the main players. But you were there. You were in his home; in his theatre, as it were: on stage, in the wings, in the audience and backstage. You saw how he acted, and you knew the cast."

"Yes. Wasn't I lucky? I met lots of his friends, mostly famous people."

"And you knew the people behind the scenes, people such as the domestic staff. They should be included."

"Well, we've all been dead for many years, so why not? And anyway, I never told you everything about them, or the Barries, or me ..."

Chapter 1

Black Lake Cottage, Tilford Road, Farnham, Surrey. That was my address for most of 1903, and my occasional place of work for a further few years. The cottage was a little nearer to the village of Tilford than Farnham, and was just within the parish of Tilford. It stood in splendid isolation in a clearing in the hilly, pine-scented woods of the Waverley Abbey estate. Situated in the lee of a narrow, steep-sided and flat-topped promontory in a sea of pine trees, the cottage was silent in its solitude except when the wind whined, and sometimes howled, through the waving trees.

Waverley Abbey House, almost a mile distant, had once been a Palladian style mansion built in the early eighteenth century from materials taken from the old Waverley Abbey nearby. After a life of over a hundred years, during which some alterations and additions were made, the house suffered from a serious fire and was largely rebuilt in 1833. The abbey was built by French monks in 1128, and it was the first Cistercian monastry established on English soil. It was home to several hundred monks and lay brothers for four hundred years until its dissolution by Henry the Eighth.

There were two lakes within the estate: a long narrow one between Waverley Abbey House and the abbey ruins, and a broader one, Black Lake, remote from the house but only a quarter of a mile downhill, through the pine-woods, from Black Lake Cottage. Whereas the first, which appeared to be a regulated, man-made feature complete with boat house, was fed from the River Wey which powered Waverley Mill and flowed through the estate, the second was in a peaty basin in the sandstone, a haven for herons and reed warblers, where the water level rose and fell at the mercy of weather and ground conditions.

For much of the time the housemaid and I had the cottage to

ourselves. We shared its large grounds with a black kitchen cat, a tethered tortoise, two white rabbits, and the gardener and his wife and young son, a small family who lived in a wooden house beyond the kitchen garden. And there were others. We all shared the garden with wild creatures - raiders from the woods, including jays and red squirrels aplenty – and sometimes with another form of life: raiding bipeds who hopefully could read, and hopefully would heed, a lone notice which pleaded, hopefully: 'Persons who come to steal the fruit are requested not to walk on the flower beds'. Finally, we shared the cottage and garden with our employers and their pet dog who were in residence from time to time, especially during the summer. For most of those periods they entertained their friends, many of them famous people from the literary and theatrical world, plus the occasional explorer or politician.

My job at the cottage was my first as a housekeeper. I was twenty-four years old when I started in May 1903. For several months before that, I had lived with my maternal grandparents, Emmanuel and Ellinor Snook, and their fifteenth and sixteenth children, my youngest uncles who were also in their twenties. That was in the hamlet of Higher Whatcombe, Dorset, where Grandfather used to be a modest farmer, having been born there on St Valentine's Day seventy five years before, and having started work as an agricultural labourer at the age of twelve. To have fathered sixteen children, he evidently was amply blessed by the patron saint of love. Grandfather had developed multiple neuritis and had been ailing for about a year after an attack of influenza. Then, in the late autumn of 1902, his health had deteriorated significantly with the onset of another bout of influenza which was to last for four months, and I had gone to his farmhouse to nurse him and help around the home. I had stayed on through the exceptionally mild February and March. Sadly, in the presence of several family members, Grandfather died on the morning of April Fools Day, which was not at all appropriate, for he was never a fool. He was buried five days later at nearby Winterborne Whitechurch after a funeral service at the Methodist Chapel where he had been a lay preacher for about fifty years. When, many years later, the chapel was pulled down, his grandchildren arranged for his memorial tablet to be affixed to the west wall in the parish church of Winterborne Whitechurch.

With the main purpose of my moving to the farmouse now gone, my grandmother soon encouraged me to seek a remunerative position somewhere.

My school education had been curtailed when, as a young teenager, I was required to stay at home to help bring up my younger brothers and sisters. After that, I had tried my hand at various occupations, both on land and at sea, and, at my father's suggestion, and with his financial support, I had trained as a Salvation Army officer, during the course of which I had acquired many skills. Useful as these were to prove throughout my life, I had decided not to make a career in the Sally Ann and so I needed to settle into some other occupation.

Within a few days, Granny found a small advertisement in the weekly newspaper which came from Winchester and always listed situations vacant in Hampshire.

"May, listen to this: 'Wanted, a young woman as housekeeper for a summer cottage. Apply: Winter, The Boynes, Medstead'. Where's Medstead?"

"I don't know, but there's one way to find out. Housekeeping appeals to me. I'll write for details."

About a week later I had secured an interview at the Royal Hotel in Winchester, about fifty miles distant. And so, early one Monday morning towards the end of April, I dressed smartly and took the pony and trap and set off down the lane to Winterborne Whitechurch, and then headed north-east, up the hill, past the Methodist Chapel, and on for five miles to Blandford Forum and the railway station, the possibility of a new job lying over the horizon.

The London & South Western Railway took me the greater part of my journey; that and shanks's pony at the other end. The longest part of my train ride was the Castleman's Corkscrew, named after the solicitor who promoted the railway between Bournemouth and Southampton. Then I had to change trains for

Winchester. I had travelled on these lines before and knew the trip would be tedious, so I took a book with me. For my birthday in January, knowing my love of books, Granny had given me a popular new novel, J. M. Barrie's *The Little White Bird*, and my journey provided an opportunity for me to make a start on it.

When I arrived at the hotel, I found two gentlemen waiting for me in the lounge. The taller one introduced himself in a Scottish accent as William Winter and then did all of the talking; he was openly warm and friendly. The other one, having been introduced to me as Mr Winter's brother-in-law, seemed similarly amicable but was quite content to sit back and simply look and listen, eyeing me as he smoked a large pipe. He was of slight build and quite short, maybe five feet two inches, with a pale complexion, and he had black hair and a moustache. His eyes were large and blue and a touch melancholy. Worryingly, he had an occasional but persistent cough, although it was not quite so loud as to interfere with the conversation. I remember wondering if he was ill, but then why would he have come here today? Later, I learned that his cough was a residual effect of his having suffered, almost fatally, from a prolonged attack of pleurisy and pneumonia while on a visit to his mother in Kirriemuir in Scotland.

After a few pleasantries to put me at my ease, Mr Winter invited me to join them both as their guest for lunch and I accepted gratefully, for it had been a long time since my breakfast. We moved to the dining room where I was given a seat opposite the two gentlemen. I placed my handbag on the floor and my book upon the table, still blissfully unaware of the identity of the second man, and the dialogue with Mr Winter continued.

The meal was a leisurely affair, a protracted conversation between occasional mouthfuls, during which I gradually revealed details of my family and my upbringing in Poole and Hackney, my teenage years in Sutton and East Dulwich, and my Salvation Army training at Clapton Training College. I explained that the training resulted in my being commissioned as a field officer and, after a spell at Portmadog, being transferred to a worship centre at Bangor, North Wales, where I was soon given the rank of Captain.

I told my interviewers that my father, James Robert Llewellyn, had been a grocer and tea merchant and also a lay preacher for the Wesleyan Church. He had gone on to become one of the first senior officers of the Salvation Army and worked with William Booth in London, where he helped found the first training college, which was in Hackney. His Pembrokeshire-born father had been a sea captain carrying Welsh slate from Portmadog to Newfoundland, returning with salt cod to Poole, and then taking manufactured goods to Portmadog.

My mother, Bessie, was the daughter of Emmanuel Snook, an evangelist and agricultural worker who was associated with Joseph Arch, the Warwickshire farm labourer who was a Primitive Methodist lay preacher and a great campaigner for rural social justice. Arch started work at the age of nine as a bird scarer and later developed skills in hedging, ditching and mowing. He went on to found the Farm Workers Union in 1872, and later became a Member of Parliament. Emmanuel went with Joseph Arch on visits to almost every town and village in Dorset, and he spoke at meetings. Through this connection, Emmanuel was known slightly to Thomas Hardy who was born just a few miles from Winterborne Whitechurch. Emmanuel's father, also a Dorset farm worker, was a friend and supporter of the Tolpuddle Martyrs; in March 1834 he marched his children down to the main road to salute them as they were being taken in chains from the Dorchester assizes to Southampton for transportation to Australia for seven years.

My family history and connections seemed to be of interest to my hosts, and at my mention of Hardy the smaller man's sad eyes widened slightly and he soon joined in the conversation. It was now evident that, like his brother-in-law, he, too, was a Scotsman. From that moment on, the talk was only of the Dorset author, and Dorset life and Dorset countryside. This gentleman was clearly an admirer of Hardy. My confidence grew somewhat because I was on home ground now, and because I had read most of Hardy's novels and poetry. Our conversation became quite protracted, not at all how I expected an interview should be conducted, and I was asked to describe in detail what life was like on my grandfather's farm.

And then came the revelation. I was stopped short when the smaller man stretched out his hand across the table, picked up my book, pointed to the author's name on the cover and said, quite solemnly, "That's me."

For what seemed like minutes but, in reality, was probably no more than a few seconds, I could not recall a single detail of what I had said since arriving at the hotel, even though I had done most of the talking. I was dumbfounded. These two had heard a good deal of my life story, yet suddenly I realised I knew almost nothing about one of them, and that the other was J. M. Barrie the writer - the famous novelist and dramatist who lived and worked and socialised in London, and who doubtless moved in the same lofty circles as other famous and wealthy people all the time.

Oh dear! Ought I to have recognised him? Would I now not be interviewed for the job? Or was this the interview, and had I just failed some cunning test? Why hadn't Barrie revealed his identity to me earlier instead of allowing me to ramble on about Thomas Hardy who very probably was a friend of his? What foolish things had I said?

But wait. What on earth was the shy Mr Barrie doing here in this Winchester hotel, albeit a rather grand one, keeping his brother-in-law company while the latter recruited a housekeeper? Surely he had far more important things to do with his time.

Involuntary expressions of puzzlement, confusion and panic must have swept across my face as suspicions of trickery grew within my mind. Mercifully, my agonising was brought to an end by the recruiter almost as quickly as it had been inadvertently initiated by his aider and abetter.

"I'm so sorry, Miss Llewellyn. It is Mr and Mrs Barrie who require a housekeeper. They have a country cottage near Farnham, about fifteen miles up the line from my home, and they had entrusted to me the job of finding a suitable person. As things turned out, Mr Barrie was down for the weekend and then visited his sister and me and, as he didn't have to be back in London until this evening, I asked him to come along today."

So that was it. I had been deceived, harmlessly but by no means charmlessly, by these gentlemen who at no time had mentioned the purpose of my journey to Winchester. I felt I had no choice but to forgive them immediately and, still wondering whether I had indeed failed their crucial test, seized the opportunity to let Mr Barrie know how much I was enjoying *The Little White Bird* and to ask him a few questions about it. Then, sensing that I might be in danger of outstaying my welcome, especially as no questions had been asked of me about my qualifications for the post, I explained that I should be going and thanked my hosts for the lunch. They accompanied me to the exit and, as I stood on the steps in the hall, ready to leave, I ventured to enquire of Mr Barrie whether I suited his requirements.

"Oh," said he, rather off-handedly but not at all unpleasantly, "consider yourself engaged and come to us next week."

And with that, and a smiling assurance from Mr Winter that he would write confirming the post and enclosing directions, I, Mabel Bessie Llewellyn, shook the hands of James Matthew Barrie and William Henderson Winter, and departed. Clutching my now very special volume, I walked on air all the way back along St Peter Street and up the hill to the railway station. It might have been raining for all I noticed.

Chapter 2

The following Monday morning saw me back on The Long & Slow Winding Railway, this time at the breezy, waterside Poole station where my mother and father had come to see me off. I had left Higher Whatcombe and returned for a few days to the family home in Poole, an Edwardian house named Mayflower, which was number 83, Longfleet Road. I had needed to sort and pack my essential belongings, and purchase some suitable new clothes and shoes, and now I was on my way to start my new job in Surrey.

I found a seat on the train, near to where my parents were standing, and released the wide, brown leather window strap on the door, thereby allowing the window to drop noisily to its lowest position. After a minute of stunted, superficial exchanges, none of which hadn't been said more meaningfully during the five minutes while we had awaited the arrival of my train, the guard's whistle cut through the noise, signalling, as it always did, the moment to actually say goodbye. A few seconds later the guard waved his green flag, hopped back on to the train, and the long, sharply curving platform and everyone on it started, barely perceptibly, to slide smoothly away from me. So gentle yet assured was the powerful pull of the giant green steam locomotive as it hissed and chugged, tugging its long, heavy train of pale salmon and dark brown coloured coaches out of the station. After waving goodbye to my receding parents I yanked the window up and settled into my seat, feeling sad at leaving Poole but excited about the next phase of my life.

Meanwhile, at the Vaudeville Theatre in London, Barrie's *Quality Street*, with Ellaline Terriss in the leading role, had been running for over seven months and, at the Duke of York's Theatre *The Admirable Crichton*, with Gerald du Maurier, had been playing for six months, both to full houses and great acclaim. Many parents might have found some amusing things to say about their daughter going off to work for someone wealthy and famous, but not mine. Oh, they were very pleased for me that I was to be housekeeper to J. M. Barrie but, at the same time, they could not refrain from voicing their concerns at the sort of people and behaviour I might encounter. They were like that; heavily moralistic. Father, now sixty-eight, retired and asthmatic, had been a magistrate and an ardent temperance advocate, striving to oppose the granting of any new licences for the sale of alcohol in Poole. His father had told him about how his own father, had drunk away all his money in Little Newcastle, Pembrokeshire. Mother felt similarly about the evil alcohol, perhaps more so, for her father had not only been a Methodist preacher but also one of the pioneers of the temperance movement in Dorset. She felt strongly also about young men showing an interest in her daughters. Woe betide any such man who didn't measure up to her stringent and moral standards; any daughter of hers who might fall in love with one and foolishly seek her approval of him could think again!

Two miles beyond the now familiar Winchester station, my train branched sharply right, off the original main line to London, and followed a more easterly route towards the capital, a single track line for part of its length, which passed through Alresford, Alton and Farnham. On the way, I noticed the train stopped at Medstead, where the Winters lived. I didn't know it then but I was to get to know that little hilltop station and its staff quite well. Three more stops, and I stepped down on to the platform at Farnham, from where I could see that the town lay on the far side of the river which the railway had followed since leaving Alton about ten miles back. A porter retrieved my trunk, which had been put off the train, and barrowed it out and down to the station forecourt where he summoned a lone waiting hackney for me. Mr Winter had told me that my destination lay about one and a half miles away. I gave the driver the address.

"Black Lake Cottage, Miss? That'll be Mr Barrie's place, then," he said, unnecessarily. "I've carried Mr and Mrs Barrie there a few times. They sometimes come down by train. Such lovely people, they are. Mr Barrie doesn't say much, though. And as for Mrs Barrie, well, she's the one of the prettiest ladies I've ever seen."

Once out of the station, we turned right, uphill, over the level crossing, and then right, into Tilford Road. The Waverley Arms, on the left, and the stationmaster's house and a string of about thirty other houses on the right, were soon left behind as the driver coaxed his horse up a long slope into the Surrey countryside. For about a mile there were small hedged fields on either side and, here and there, growing out of the roadside hedges, were many large deciduous trees, mostly oaks, their leaves as yet unfurled. On a crest in the road a sign indicated that Greenhill Farm lay a short distance along a track leading off to the right.

"This is Green Hill, Miss," the driver told me. Then, with what I thought was a sheepish grin, he added, "The farmer at Greenhill Farm, just over there, is Henry Lamb". I expect he told that to all his passengers.

Less effort was required of the horse as the road began to go downhill. Passing between high banks, it went round and down, over a stream, where we entered woodland, and then it was round and up a short hill where there was a cross roads.

"This is Red Hill, Miss. By the way, the road on the left is the way to Waverley Abbey House and the abbey ruins," and then we went downhill again, past a farm on the left, and then a pair of cottages on the right, and on until the dusty, golden yellow sandstone road rose a little before levelling off. We were now deep in woods of Scots pine. I had just started remarking to my driver about the colourful landscape hereabouts, particularly the hills, when he slowed his trotting horse, steered him right, through an open white gate, and stopped beside a white-walled house which had reddish-brown roofs, green doors, and green window frames and shutters. Each shutter had a small heart-shaped hole cut in it, doubtless a woman's touch. So this was Black Lake Cottage. Hardly a cottage, I thought, for it seemed a fair size and not at all what I had expected. A woman approached me from farther up the drive.

"Hello, you must be Miss Llewellyn. We had a letter telling us to expect you today. Ask the driver to set your trunk and suitcase down there. My husband will help you in with them later. I'm Jessie Cane, and my husband, William, is the gardener. We have a son, John, who helps his dad in the garden sometimes, but he's at school down in Tilford just now. He's only nine. I expect you'd like a cup of tea after your long journey."

I paid the driver my fare, adding a small tip, which I imagined was rather less than he was accustomed to receiving from Mr Barrie, and followed Jessie up the drive.

"We've been here three years now," continued Jessie, as we passed the back corner of the cottage. I looked to my left and caught a glimpse of part of the garden. Immediately behind the cottage, standing on a brick paved area, was a large green kennel with its back to the wall.

"That used to be Porthos's kennel," explained Jessie. "He died over a year ago."

"He must have been a large dog. Why, a man could almost crawl inside that."

"Mr Barrie, maybe, but my William would have a job," joked Jessie. "That's Luath's bed now. He's still a puppy but he's quite a size already. Come on, this way."

The drive curved sharply to the right, ran by a coach house, and then narrowed and curved gently the other way.

"Mrs Barrie engaged William when she took the place over from Henry Lewis, the London jeweller. Mr Lewis's wife, Anna, died, and his daughter, Jane, was often away from home, and he didn't want to remain here alone after that. I'm afraid he let the place go a little. He moved to Ealing and we heard he married a much younger woman."

There were kitchen gardens behind low hedges to either side of the drive. Ahead, I could see some greenhouses and a row of cold frames. Just as Jessie was telling me that she was originally from Nairn, in Scotland, a jay skaaked past unmelodiously, chased by a couple of smaller birds.

"I wonder what he's done to upset them?" I asked.

"Oh, we get a lot of jays in the garden. I never saw any back home, though. There's no shortage of wildlife here," said Jessie as she led me through the door of her small wooden house at the edge of the garden. "Sit yourself down at the table and I'll make the tea. The kettle's already on. It's always on for William. The cottage is really Mrs Barrie's, you know, not Mr Barrie's," she continued. "She's leased it from the Waverley Estate. She's the one who's really in charge here. She soon made changes to the place, and I don't think she's finished yet. There's been builders here twice already, and painters and decorators, inside and out. It's bigger and brighter than it was. And as for the garden, well that's larger too, nearly three acres now. It was less than two acres when we came here. There's about eight acres altogether; the rest of it is pinewoods. Listen: can you hear that? That's William at work with his saw now. I don't know how many trees have been felled but there's been no shortage of logs for the fires, I can tell you. William's never worked so hard in his life, what with putting up fences and posts, building paths and courtyards, and carrying out a hundred-and-one other ideas Mrs Barrie keeps coming up with. Last year he had to dig out a ravine and line it with large boulders and steps. Mind you, she did most of the planting in it. She calls it her sunk garden. She certainly seems to know what she's doing, and she wants the garden to be even larger. She's been talking about building ponds, and a stream with bridges. William and I, we wonder where it will end, and so does Mr Barrie, I should think. Rupert Anderson, the gentleman who owns Waverley, he must be a very tolerant man. Milk?"

"Yes, please. Give her an inch and she'll take a mile, then," I interjected, hoping for a chance to get a word in, for Jessie seemed unstoppable also.

"Exactly. William says that old George Hunt, that was Mr Lewis's gardener, must have had it pretty easy towards the end. All he had to do was keep the smaller garden tidy, and it seems he wasn't too good at that towards the end. Still, he was seventy-seven when he finished. His daughter, Kate, was the cook, and she left at the same time and went to a new position in Brighton."

"I gather Mr and Mrs Barrie aren't at home."

"No, I think they're back here next weekend."

That was good to know. Jessie had just confirmed what Mr Winter had said in his letter to me a few days earlier, and it pleased me because it meant I would have plenty of time to settle in and get organised.

"Sugar?"

"No, thanks, Jessie."

"There you are, then. We'll soon have you feeling at home."

"Thank you. Mr Winter, that's Mr Barrie's brother-in-law, he told me there's a housemaid here," I said, beginning to wonder if I was going to be living on my own in the cottage. Having noticed the size of the place, I was feeling a bit apprehensive about what the household held in store for me.

"Yes, that's Alice. She lives with her parents and grandfather just a few hundred yards up the road in one of the pair of cottages they call Black Lake, which is a bit confusing, what with this being called Black Lake Cottage. You passed the cottages on the way. Ever since they left school, both Alice and her elder sister, Fanny, were housemaids for the Lewises. Alice told me she and Fanny used to live here all the time in those days. The Barries took them on because they were highly recommended by Mr Lewis, and also because they were the only housemaids within a mile of here. You see, the Barries needed them to live here only when they themselves were here. At other times, when there was nothing like as much work for them to do, the girls could live at home and just pop along here for a few hours a day. They got paid full wages, of course, otherwise they'd have found work elsewhere. Then, last December, Fanny got married to her young man, Alfie Embleton, and she moved away, leaving Alice to look after the place on her own through the winter. Alice hasn't been too happy about that since Mr and Mrs Barrie started coming down again, so she's been looking forward to your arrival."

A little later that afternoon, I moved in to my room upstairs at the rear of the house. The view from its small, south facing, gable end window was of a large, perfectly flat, rectangular lawn between long herbaceous borders. To the right, running along behind the border, was a grassed avenue of young trees and, beyond that, I could see part of a sloping landscaped garden. Beyond everything there was woodland. Some deciduous trees straight ahead, and then pines everywhere. I opened the window and leaned out to gain a wider view. To the right, there was more lawn. Lots of it, sloping gently up towards the woods, dotted here and there with shrubs and small trees. And beyond that was a steep pine-clad hill. Jessie Cane was right: this garden was huge. Below me was a stone-paved courtyard with clumps of lavender and a sundial on a pedestal, the whole enclosed by a yew hedge. Looking left, I could see some of the west side of the cottage. The older parts on the first floor had mainly sliding sash windows with large window panes, while the recent additions had casements with small leaded panes. The leads were painted white. The woodwork was white except for the window surrounds which, like the shutters, were painted green. All the walls were rendered and painted white. Nearest to me there was a ground floor extension with a flat roof. I decided to explore the cottage.

Although the domestic staff had their own staircase, evidently a recent addition on the north side, all of the upstairs rooms were accessible from both staircases as there was a long zigzag passage connecting the two. Progressing along the passage I found three guest bedrooms, a dressing room and a luxurious, white tiled bathroom on the left side, and, on the right, two windows giving a south view of the garden, and two windows giving a west view. The door to the main bedroom was right by the top of the stairs, at the far end of the passage. This room had east and west aspects and a doorway, without a door, leading to an adjoining smaller room beyond. This appeared to be a recent addition, with a new fireplace, and it was obviously the dressing room of the lady of the house.

The main staircase descended into a large hall with a fireplace. Through a small porch was the front door; it was quite a modest entrance for such wealthy people. To the right was a door which opened into a large, airy, L-shaped drawing room. Straight ahead, in an extended portion of the room, there was a new brick fireplace of unusual corbelled design and without a mantlepiece. I'd never seen one like it before. To my right, French windows afforded access to the garden through a shady and substantial canopy. The most striking and unexpected feature was a wide, inward curving window in the inner angle of the L. This faced roughly south-west and so allowed additional light into the centre of the essentially pale green room which was already illuminated by the light from windows of various sizes in three of its six walls. A number of differently patterned carpets and rugs covered most of the floor, and the curtains and some seat covers were of a bold chintz which was repeated in a frieze.

Returning to the hall, I saw that it also served as a sitting room. There was a high-backed wing chair to one side of the fireplace; this proved to be Mr Barrie's favourite seat in the cottage, a place for thinking. The room extended back as a dining hall with lots of uncurtained, small-paned window, and there was a door at the far end giving access to the courtyard below my own window. Alice later told me that the extension replaced a conservatory, and that, beyond the conservatory there had been a lean-to which Mrs Barrie had detested. In contrast to the drawing room, here in the dining hall the carpet was a plain blue and it extended right up to the walls. Close to the narrow, extending, Tudor style dining table and its eight blue-cushioned chairs, a side door took me directly into the kitchen where I was a little alarmed to find that the range, a close fire range with oven and boiler, was immediately on my left. I imagined that noisy activities in here could easily intrude upon conversation at the table just a few feet away. Clearly, that was something for me to worry about.

The kitchen was light and airy. It's only window faced north but it was a wide one giving a good view of the drive, and of a tall laurel hedge which screened the lower kitchen garden from the cottage and its visitors. This room had unglazed red floor tiles and was extremely well equipped, as one might expect, with high quality modern equipment and utensils. Under the window were two large sinks, and beside one of these was a hand pump which, I soon learned, produced high quality, soft water from an underground tank fed by a spring in the garden. How convenient. It would save much time and effort not having to go outside in all weathers to fetch water in buckets and jugs; we could fill them in here. Through a door to the right was the servants' room, which included a large store cupboard containing cleaning equipment including a carpet sweeper. This room also had the tradesmen's entrance which was accessible from the drive. On the other side of the end wall was the coal store, forming the corner of the cottage, but accessible only from the outside. From the opposite end of the kitchen, another door led through the scullery, past the pantry on the left, to an exit to the back garden and, to the right, a short passage led to the servants hall and the servants staircase, all fairly new. But where was the cellar?

It was plain to see that the cottage had been enlarged several years ago by a previous owner to provide what was now the kitchen, the servants room and coal store, and the bathroom and two bedrooms above. It had then been further enlarged quite recently, though again not all in one massive operation, for some of the beams, doors and windows looked fairly new while others, like some of the paintwork, looked brand new. The cellar, if indeed there was one, most probably would have formed part of the original building, and therefore would be beneath either what was now the sitting room or the drawing room, both of which, unlike the kitchen, had a wooden floor. A closer look revealed the entrance to the cellar, and a quick inspection confirmed that it was in use for cool storage.

Throughout the house the walls and ceilings were of white distemper, thus conspiring to lighten and brighten all the rooms. Most carpets, rugs and soft furnishings were either green or blue, some plain, some patterned. Here and there was purple and deep red, but I noticed that yellow was conspicuouly absent. I soon learned that the only yellow-coloured features which Mrs Barrie would allow in the house were floral displays and, unless specially requested in advance of her arrival, these were created by her, and her alone.

Everything was finished and maintained to a very high standard, and the comforable rooms were filled with all sorts of elegant furniture, ornate wall lamps, ceiling lamps, standard lamps and table lamps, many paintings, photographs, brasses, coppers, ornaments and mirrors, including several circular convex mirrors. Many items were hung high up on the walls. Clearly there was no shortage of dusting, cleaning and polishing work in this house.

Having seen round the interior of the whole building, I could not resist going back upstairs for another look at the large garden. The main staircase was illuminated by light from a window not quite opposite the top – for on the wall there were Japanese prints and a small mirror - but a few feet to the right, opposite a landing. The upper of the two sliding sash windows incorporated an attractive semicircular arch of Victorian design with panes of different coloured glass. This window faced slightly south of west and so, on sunny afternoons, the colourful arch design was projected obliquely on to the white wall and door of one of the bedrooms, a room which, I discovered a little later, was used by Mr Barrie not only as a separate bedroom but doubled as a dressing room and a minimally equipped study.

The window was adjacent to one corner of the flat roof which, I now knew, covered the dining hall. What I didn't know, however, was that in a few years' time this window would be replaced with a door, the door to a new study which Mrs Barrie would have built above the dining hall. The study would be airy and bright because it would have no ceiling and there would be two very large bowed windows, and there would be a plain black carpet which would be the very devil for someone to keep looking clean and free from the black and white hairs from a certain large pet, and the blue-grey fur from a smaller one. The other windows in the passage would be blocked off, throwing the passage into darkness, but a small new window, near the far end, would be inserted to allow some light in via the study, and to allow a discreet view into the study from the passage, and the door to the study would be half-glazed. Mr Barrie's earlier wish to have his study up in the pine woods, instead, would not be granted. Why, I never knew, but did this contribute to his idea to have Wendy's house built among the trees in *Peter Pan*?

Still standing near the top of the stairs, I slid the lower window up as far as it would go, and leaned out to enjoy a west-facing view of the beautiful garden, a first-floor view which one day would be denied to all visitors unless invited into the study, or into Mrs Barrie's bedroom. Apart from the songs of garden and woodland birds, it was blissfully quiet. I stayed at that sunny window for a long time, absorbing the atmosphere and the stillness of the place.

So this was the home, but what of the people? How would I get on with the author and his wife? What interesting visitors would I meet?

Chapter 3

April had been a cold month, colder than March, which was highly unusual, and therefore this year's spring had been firmly repressed for a few weeks. May was much warmer, however, and brought all the deciduous trees fully into leaf within days of each other as nature rapidly made up for lost time.

It was now apparent that there were many silver birches, here and there, beside the paths and tracks running through the surrounding woods. Farther afield, welcome bright green patches of new foliage betrayed the presence of larger deciduous trees, including oaks and beeches, abutting the dark monotony of the pines.

The cottage garden, too, became greener and more colourful, with pink and blue hues breaking up the monopoly of late winter's whites and yellows. The expansive grassed areas and paths – more than an acre in total - started once more to present William and his boy assistant with an increased demand for mowing. The long lawn to the south of the cottage was cut closer than the other areas, and William told me the reason for this: it had always to be in a fit state for games of golf-croquet, one of Mr Barrie's passions. This required that the lawn had also to be rolled.

Alice Joyce Lamport was just a year older than me and excellent at her job. She had been working at the cottage for about twelve years and, like me, had also become an accomplished cook. Alice told me that, in addition to a long summer stay, Mr Barrie and Mrs Barrie visited the cottage for several weekends, and the occasional week, each year. Sometimes only one of them came. If it was Mrs Barrie, it would be to see William and tend to the garden, or it would be to meet builders to discuss some improvement proposal. All the changes to both the cottage and its garden had been at her instigation and to her requirements and designs. Before she married the author,

Mary Ansell had been a moderately successful actress and had run her own touring company, as well as appearing on the stage in London's West End. Six years after having given up working, she had found that the acquisition of the cottage provided a new outlet for her creativity, the more so because the marriage had not resulted in any children. When present, Mrs Barrie spent a lot of her time in the garden and did some of the lighter work herself. Among her favourite flowers were delphiniums, roses, carnations and sweet peas.

The delphiniums, hundreds of them, were ranged across a border on the higher ground such that, in the sunlight especially, their slender, striking blue spikes contrasted with the shady backdrop of the pine woods. Tea roses were grouped in small beds set in the upper lawn, while crimson ramblers stretched in a long line just a few feet below the delphinium border. The upper kitchen garden was divided from the orchard by a long rose hedge, while an adjacent side was bordered by a path, along both sides of which grew the sweet peas. In the angle between the rose hedge and the sweet peas there was a square patch for growing carnations. These and the sweet peas were grown in large quantities and were regularly cut for display; mauve and purple sweet peas in small copper vases were always in evidence around the cottage through the summer months. If Mrs Barrie had had to choose just one colour for her garden, I'd say it would have been blue. I think the delphiniums were closest to her heart. If she could have had everything her way with Mr Anderson, I think she would have had delphiniums marching all the way up to the top of the hill, and striding the quarter of a mile over and down to Black Lake.

The first time Mr Barrie came to the cottage since I took up my position there, he had just turned forty three. Alice and I had just finished a week-long spring-clean, during which I had tried to sort out various items which had been stored in one of the bedrooms. It was as well that he arrived when he did because I had found a tattered old box, once yellow, of the sort men used to carry their silk hats about in. It was such a dirty, ragged object that I had put it with a pile of other things for possible disposal. A little later, when I was about to take it out to William to put on the bonfire, I chanced to open it and found some yellow papers tied up in bundles inside. Better show these to Mr Barrie, I thought, and I took the box to the study which, at that time, was part of a bedroom.

"Shall I throw these away, Sir," I asked, and he gave me such a comical look.

"H'm," he began, as so often he did. The sound of this short, almost staccato utterance could have many different connotations, its nature betraying the tone of what was to follow. In this case it was unsmiling amusement. "Why, that's my Greenwood Hat-box," he said. "It was second-hand when it came to me from Scotland," and, talking between puffs and coughs, he explained how, as soon as he arrived in London as a poor young man in 1885, he had bought first a penny bottle of ink and then a silk hat just to show Frederick Greenwood, editor of the St James's Gazette, that, in spite of his nailed boots and country clothes, he was a man of the world.

It's a good thing I had not thrown the papers away, for they were some of the first articles Mr Barrie had had published when he was a beginner in journalism. The one called *The Rooks Begin to Build* was among them. He told me he had posted that one in Scotland two days before leaving there, and when he arrived at St Pancras railway station the first thing he saw was a billboard advertising it. He watched people buying the Gazette and sat down on his wooden university box and looked and looked at the placard and thought: 'I've only been in London one minute and I've made two guineas,' and, of course, his spirits went up.

Many years later, in 1930, Mr Barrie republished these early writings, linked with some of his memories, in a volume he called *The Greenwood Hat*. It was produced in a limited quantity: just fifty expensive copies for friends. In 1937, the book was published for the public. In it, Mr Barrie revealed that it was the sight of the old hat-box that stirred up his emotion more than the re-acquaintance with the papers it contained. I had to smile when I read that, for I wondered whether he would have thought to republish the articles had I not shown him the hat-box. I was amused also by his statement that the articles and the hat-box were a recent discovery because, by then, the hat-box had been lost to him for over a quarter of a century, the articles not having been returned to the box but having been placed elsewhere for safer keeping on that significant day in May 1903. What became of the hat-box? That was for William and me to know, and for you, dear reader, to ponder.

One day soon, Mr Barrie had a visitor to the cottage. It was Charles Frohman, the American theatrical producer and impresario who was hugely successful both on Broadway and in London's West End, and who did so much for the playwright. He was a rather strange, round-faced, round-bodied man but he always seemed to be happy and smiling. In addition to the business relationship between them, the two were clearly very close friends. Frohman came over to London maybe twice a year, and I met this gentle man twice. Sadly, twelve years later, he was to perish on Cunard's 'fastest and largest steamer' in Atlantic service, the *Lusitania*, when it sank off the south coast of Ireland after being torpedoed by a German U-boat.

Other famous visitors were mostly from the literary and artistic world. One of the most welcome ones was the poet George Meredith, then in his seventies, who twice drove over from his home on Box Hill. I was so excited when Mrs Barrie informed me that he was expected, for he was my favourite poet; I especially loved his *South-West Wind in the Woodland*. Mr Barrie had admired Meredith for years and, after travelling out from London to Box Hill, where he sat for hours on the bank opposite Meredith's Flint Cottage – the bank has since been named 'Barrie's Bank' - had become very close friends with him. He was also very special to Mrs Barrie, perhaps because he shared her enthusiasm for her lovely garden. Meredith was envious of the Barries because they were surrounded by pine woods. He loved all trees – his Flint House was closely bounded on three sides by deciduous woodland, and some of his poems included wonderful descriptions of trees - but pines had a special place in his heart and he loved to walk among them in all weathers. Mrs Barrie clearly thought the white-bearded, eye-twinkling, always laughing Meredith was a charming gentleman. And, from what little I saw of him, so did I.

Visitors also included the occasional politician and explorer. There was Stanley Baldwin, who later became a Conservative Prime Minister; Augustine Birrell, a Liberal politician who was also an author and who became Chief Secretary for Ireland; and Captain Robert Falcon Scott of the Royal Navy, who I met in 1906 a couple of years after his return from his first expedition to the Antarctic. The Devonian explorer was actually of Scottish descent and was one of Barrie's heroes and the two had become friends. I thought him most handsome: an alert, fit, outdoors type with penetrating blue eyes which allegedly turned to purple when he became amorous! A girl in my position could only dream, of course, and two years later Scott married Kathleen Bruce, a young Scottish sculptress. Their son Peter was a Godson of Mr Barrie, and he excelled at so many things and made his name as a painter, and was knighted for his work as a conservationist,. How could I have imagined, as I served dinner to the confident polar explorer in the cosy warmth of my master's dining hall, that in less than six years' time he and his four fellow explorers, having found they had been beaten to the South Pole just thirty-four days earlier by Amundsen and his Norwegian team, would perish from hunger and extreme cold, stranded in the frozen Antarctic landscape while attempting their eight hundred mile return journey to their base on foot? One can only wonder what other achievements might have been Robert Scott's had he survived that ill-fated second expedition.

In temperate Surrey, when our weather was fair, Mr Barrie would persuade his guests to leave the lunch table and move to the garden to play golf-croquet on the long lawn. The game was taken seriously by the host who never seemed to tire of teaching newcomers the correct way to hold the mallet and play strokes. The mallet had to be held and swung beside one's legs, never between them. So keen was he that, if it came on to rain during a game, he would insist they continued playing and would relent only if it intensified. I was reminded of Stanley Baldwin taking part in one of these games when, years later, he famously said that politicians 'resemble Alice in Wonderland, who tried to play croquet with a flamingo instead of a mallet'.

When I met Mrs Barrie for the first time I was immediately struck by her natural beauty. She was petite, a little taller than her husband, beautifully slim with a finely featured face, brown eyes and reddish-brown hair which was showing signs of greying. I had seen her engraved portrait, as Miss Mary Ansell twelve years earlier, hanging in the drawing room. She looked older now, for she was forty two – several years older than she let on - but she still wore her hair up much of the time, and I kept thinking: 'I hope I look that young when I reach her age'.

Mary Ansell was born on March 1st, 1861, in The King's Head, Bayswater, Paddington. She was the only daughter among four children of the licensed victualler, George Ansell and his wife, Mary Kitchen. All the family were Londoners. After her father had died when in his fifties, her mother retired to a house in Hastings, where she lived off the income from renting out a number of houses. While her older brothers had embarked on careers in other parts of the country – George in Birmingham, William in Bristol, and her younger brother, Thomas, a brewer's apprentice in Weedon Bec, Northamptonshire - the young Mary had moved to the south coast with her mother when in her late teens. It was from Hastings that she started out on her acting career.

Mrs Barrie was an intelligent woman, determined and efficient, with a friendly manner towards me, initially, which I warmed to instantly. As I had expected, she instructed that she was to be called Mrs Barrie or ma'am at all times. She called me either Miss Llewellyn or Mabel, depending on the circumstances, but she never called me May. That would have been too pally. Mr Barrie was just the same. All domestic staff were addressed in the same way: always proper names, never diminutive forms. That was good. I liked consistency. I liked to know where I stood.

I was surprised to discover that Mrs Barrie had not had a housekeeper before, simply housemaids and, in London, a cook. I think she, in turn, was rather taken aback to find that I had not been a housekeeper before. It was Mr Barrie, remember, who gave me the job, and, on reflection, that did seem a little strange. We soon agreed that it would be prudent to draw up a list of my responsibilities. Mrs Beeton was her guide, to which I consented – not that I felt I had any choice in the matter - and an agreed set of housekeeping rules was later hung in the kitchen and remained there for years. The rules were not strictly enforced, I might say, but there was an understanding between us that there would be recourse to them should it ever prove necessary. That Mrs Barrie might one day lay down the law, I didn't doubt, for there were certainly times when she was very direct with Alice and me, even rude on a few occasions.

At meal times Mr Barrie always sat at the far end of the long, narrow dining table, thus commanding a view down the table and across the original dining hall beyond. Mrs Barrie sat at the opposite end of the table, just six feet from the kitchen door. Their guests, never more than six for dinner, sat on the two sides. Mr Barrie preferred plain cooking, and there had always to be a large selection of fresh vegetables or salads, as well as fresh fruit. This presented no problem to me, nor to the gardener because there was nearly an acre of kitchen gardens, fruit garden, orchard and greenhouses.

Whenever Mrs Barrie was absent I carved at the table, and on those occasions I was usually brought into the conversation. I found that a little disconcerting at first; the guests were usually at least fifteen years my senior, well-known, well educated and highly literate, and I was in awe of most of them. But I convinced myself that the master had confidence in me, for he never told me so himself. I reasoned that my ability to hold an adequately intelligent conversation as a housekeeper had been demonstrated to his satisfaction at my interview. Indeed, that may well have been the overriding quality which got me the job - that and my experience in serving and caring for others, for which he only had my word. Formal qualifications and references never came into it. I found that Mr Barrie could appear very casual about some important things but that didn't always mean that he didn't care about them. Equally, he could be terribly serious, sometimes almost frighteningly so, about details which would be of little consequence to many people. And at such times his stare could kill at twenty paces, while his vowel-growling voice would rise in both pitch and volume as he emphasised his consonants. He may have been shy, short in stature, and light in weight, but he did not lack presence in a room and he was not a person to be underestimated. No sir!

Carving at lunch and dinner enabled me to meet one of the master's greatest literary friends, Thomas Hardy. By then, Hardy was in his mid sixties, a fairly shy man who was born and still lived in my home county. A few years earlier he had finished with writing novels after a lot of fuss was raised over *Jude The Obscure* when people accused him of attacking the sanctity of marriage. He had previously suffered a hostile review of *Tess of the D'Urbervilles* and had made it clear then that a continuation of such attacks would lead him to cease novel-writing. He was now exclusively a poet and I already had a copy of his *Wessex Poems* among my books. The master had told him I was from Dorset, and that prompted Hardy to talk to me with a broad 'Doarset' accent, using 'Dialect words – those terrible marks of the beast to the truly genteel' to tell me that his mother had been a domestic servant and a great lover of literature, and that she had instilled in him a love of books from an early age. When he found that I had spent some months living at Higher Whatcombe, he asked after my grandfather and the farm, for he didn't know that Grandfather had died. He explained that he had studied the plight of rural labourers and had taken an interest in the activities of Joseph Arch because he felt it important that writers and artists should understand actual situations and describe and comment upon them. He had even heard Grandfather speaking at a public meeting. I could hardly believe it! About twenty years later, while shopping in Dorchester, I spotted an elderly but evidently still very fit and healthy Thomas

Hardy in the street and I made so bold as to introduce my two children to him. To Topsy and Jim's astonishment, and mine, that lovely gentleman remembered me immediately.

Chapter 4

The most important social event on the Black Lake Cottage calendar was the annual cricket week. It brought many visitors to the cottage. Mr Barrie was a very keen, though not highly accomplished cricketer, and he captained his own team called the Allahakbarries, the name being a play on an Arabic word and his surname and meaning Heaven help Barrie's team. This name was quite apt for, speaking about his performance in one two-innings match, Barrie once said, amusingly: "The first time I scored one run, the second time I was not so lucky". His players were mainly authors, some having little or no previous knowledge or experience of the game, and at the beginning of July each year the team played a match against Sir Edgar Horne's team on an exclusive ground at Hall Place, Shackleford. Also in July, from 1903 to 1905, and two or three days following the Shackleford match, they played a team of artists, a team got up by some artists living nearby at Frensham. There were one or two games played elsewhere in the southern counties, usually in May or June, but Black Lake Cottage was not conveniently located to be used as a base on those occasions.

For the cricket weeks the Allahakbarries team descended on the cottage on or about the last day of June and practised on the long lawn. In some cases, it was necessary for the captain to introduce new recruits to the cricket bat and how to hold it. I didn't know much about cricket but I knew enough to wonder how Mr Barrie could be a right-handed batsman and croquet player and yet bowl with his left arm. It turned out that he was ambidextrous and his specialism was in bowling left-arm googlies. He had a bat which was given to him by C. B. Fry, the England test cricketer, although I doubt if any of Fry's renowned skill transferred itself to its second owner despite the Scottish batsman's revered boldness at the wicket.

During the cricket weeks there was also a golf-croquet

tournament at the cottage, and on days when there was no cricket match or golf-croquet tournament, people would go walking in the woods, or simply eat, drink and converse in the cottage and in the garden. Or, more or less willingly, they would submit to playing more golf-croquet.

The cricket weeks, normally more like very long weekends, meant a lot of extra work for the domestic staff. Several of the gentlemen brought their wives, and the cottage was full to overflowing for several days. While Mr Barrie directed his energies toward the games, Mrs Barrie concerned herself with making sure all the guests were welcomed and well catered for.

There was never room for everyone to stay at the cottage and so most of the visitors were found accommodation in Farnham and a few in Tilford. This at least limited the workload for us at breakfast but, while providing breakfast for eight people, seated at 9.30am, was one thing, catering for twenty or more for lunch, tea and dinner was quite another. We provided banquets in the garden often on these occasions. On the lawn William had to erect both a large tent with awnings, and also a long table from trestles and boards which we would cover with several white tablecloths. The positions for these were dictated by Mr Barrie, naturally, to ensure that there was no encroachment on to the croquet playing area.

Mrs Barrie was very specific as to what food and drink was to be served each day, and she would send detailed instructions by letter from London about a week beforehand, so that I could organise everything in good time. I would discuss with the gardener my schedule of daily requirements for vegetables, salads, herbs and fruit, and any items he would not be able to provide from the kitchen gardens would be added to my huge shopping list. Much of what was required would be ordered from the various roundsmen from retailers in Farnham who called at the cottage on their scheduled days. For other items, I would cycle or beg a ride into Farnham to place orders and specify delivery dates with various shopkeepers. I especially remember having to visit several times the draper's shop in The Borough; this was owned by Alfred Bentall, an Essex man whose first shop was in Sittingboune in Kent, but he moved his business to Farnham. His son, Charles, eventually took over and continued expanding the business. Bentalls grew rapidly into a very large concern with their main department store at Kingston upon Thames, where my son and his family lived many years later.

Preparing and serving the food and drinks, and clearing away and washing up, was a continuous operation during these special occasions, for everything had to be fresh or freshly cooked. And there were similar unusually high demands with respect to all the other domestic work. Alice and I couldn't possibly have coped without additional help, and that help always came in the shape of two or three more ladies, domestic staff from the Barries' main residence, Leinster Corner, in Kensington.

My first experience of a Black Lake Cricket Week was in 1903, when I had been in my post for a mere two months. It had been an exciting prospect but also a daunting one. Thank heavens for Mitchell Shand, Mary Atkins and Annie Gosling that year. Mitchell was the Barries' cook, a thirty-three year old farmer's daughter from Banff in Scotland. Once she arrived I was only too glad to bow to her greater experience and expertise, for she had catered for large numbers here before. And besides, she knew all Mrs Barrie's preferences whereas I had only just met the hostess. Mary was a parlourmaid, a Londoner who was a little younger than Mitchell. Annie was a housemaid from Oxfordshire, another farmer's daughter, and she was much younger.

Annie Gosling and I were the same age. Annie was really her middle name; her first name was Esther but she didn't like it to be used. She wasn't terribly happy about her surname either. When some folks heard that she was a farmer's daughter they would make jokes about goslings hatching out on the farm and would ask her why, when she grew up, she hadn't changed her name to Goose. She needn't have worried, though, because she was well liked by the Barries; her elder sister, Jane – actually Mary Jane – had been a housemaid to them earlier, and when Annie was old enough to work they took her on as well. Jane left her job when she married Edward Goldsmith in 1898. And as for

Annie changing her surname, when cupid's arrow finally struck she married a gander named Thomas Archer.

There was one other person on hand to help around the place during the cricket weeks, and he was known to us as Fred. To Mr and Mrs Barrie, however, he was always Frederick - 'the elegant Frederick', in fact, which I took to be a term of endearment following on from Barrie's current successful play *The Admirable Crichton*. He was their chauffeur appointed, at about the same time as me, to drive their new car, a Lanchester. In five years time, and after I had left the Barries' employ, Frederick would be replaced by 'the splendid Alphonse'. Perhaps those terms reflected the chauffeurs' superior knowledge and expertise with motor cars, and their ability to take charge in the event of their passengers becoming marooned on a lonely highway? I often wondered whether any flattering descriptive term had been allocated to my name and, if so, what it was. Of one thing I was sure: I was an excellent cook, and the Barries acknowledged that. But what of my other qualities? Perhaps that was something best left. After all, the first chauffeur, Alfred, did not seem to have had a prefix, not as far as Alice knew, anyway, and he lasted only two years. Maybe he was not so great.

During the cricket weeks Fred spent much of his time driving members of the Allahakbarries and their ladies to and from the grounds where their matches were played, and also between their places of accommodation and Black Lake Cottage. Tilford Road saw more of that Lanchester in that one week than in the whole of the remainder of the year.

Fred told Alice and me that Mr Barrie had taken delivery of the car in May, having ordered it some weeks earlier following a test drive with the Lanchester Company's chief demonstrator, Archibald Millarship, and that he had done this on the recommendation of Rudyard Kipling. Like Kipling and Millarship, Barrie owned a 1900 steam-car built by the English Locomobile Company based in Kensington, but all three had grown tired of the vehicle's short range and unreliability, and had come to regard it as little more than a large toy. The petrol-engined 'twenty-four-horse Octopod' which 'sang like a six inch shell' and possessed 'a horn that has no duplicate in all the Home Counties', as Kipling described his 1901 Lanchester in his *Steam Tactics*, was altogether a far better proposition. Fred boasted that 'she' could reach thirty miles per hour and travel over two hundred miles on a tank of petrol. She? Thirty miles per hour? No-one's allowed to go more than fourteen miles per hour! Whatever next? We had no idea how motor cars would advance, nor how they would proliferate as they became ever more affordable.

Mr Barrie's Lanchester, like Kipling's, also was a 1901 model, an open top one which he and Mrs Barrie would ride in only when the weather was dry. Consequently, they had not made much use of it during June of 1903 because the month had been very cold, and the middle portion had been extremely wet in London where there had been serious flooding. Fred had driven Mr Barrie and a guest down to Black Lake Cottage in the car just once before, but that had been a short visit and I had seen Fred only long enough to give him a cup of tea and something to eat. This time it was different, and I began to get to know him a little.

The Lanchester was garaged in the coach house just a few yards from the back of the cottage. Some years later, however, it was parked in the gardener's wooden house which was converted for the purpose following a Surrey County Council planning order stipulating that the building was not to be used as a dwelling. The gardener and his family were rehoused in the coach house following its approved conversion into a dolls house of a home.

It seemed to Fred that Mr Barrie wasn't enamoured with the Lanchester. It was mainly Mrs Barrie who used it, while her husband preferred walking or taking a cab. It wasn't that the Lanchester had anything wrong with it. Far from it, for clearly it was a beautiful machine admired by many. Mr Barrie just didn't like cars. Perhaps he had alarming visions of what was to come, but there was no doubting his appreciation of it when it came to transporting his guests, especially the members of his cricket team.

Mrs Barrie always supplied me with a list of names of those

invited to the cricket weeks. A number of ladies were invited in their own right, rather than as partners of the cricketers; these were mainly actresses who had acted in the master's plays. I vividly remember meeting the American Ethel Barrymore in 1905. She was just a few months younger than me and incredibly beautiful. It was no wonder that she became an idol of young girls who copied her voice, her walk and several other of her mannerisms. I noticed that she and Captain Harry Graham, one of the cricketer guests, seemed to spend a lot of time together while at the cottage. They also had rooms at the same inn in Farnham. While Miss Barrymore's stay at Farnham was not reported in the local newspaper, it was not long before there were rumours spreading about the possibility of marriage. But personalities like Barrymore always attracted such attention. She was also supposed to be marrying several other British men during the early nineteen hundreds, including Prince Ranjitsinjhi, the British-Indian cricketer, and Gerald du Maurier, the actor, but she was not long in Britain and she returned to America later in 1905 to take the leading role in Barrie's *Alice Sit-by-the-Fire*, both on Broadway and on tour, and four years later she married an American.

I remember most of the gentlemen players: The novelist Maurice Hewlett, for example, came every year while I was there, bringing with him his wife Hilda who, in 1911, was to become the first woman in the country to obtain a pilot's licence; Owen Seaman, editor of Punch magazine, who later became known also as a World War 1 poet, and whose Goddaughter married A. A. Milne, the creator of Pooh Bear having met her through becoming assistant editor at Punch; E. V. Lucas, writer who, on his second visit, in 1905, brought his wife, (Florence) Elizabeth, and daughter Audrey – in fact they arrived a fortnight earlier and, together with the Hewletts, made quite a holiday of it; Walter Frith, novelist; Charles Turley Smith, writer and critic; A. E. W. Mason, novelist and writer of short stories, most famous for *The Four Feathers*; H. B. Marriott Watson, a New Zealander who had emigrated to Britain and who wrote novels and short stories, especially ones of a swashbuckling nature such as *The Privateers* and *Hurricane Island* - Marriott Watson was married to the poet and literary and art critic, Rosamund Ball, a divorced woman who wrote under the pseudonym of Graham R. Tomson and was regarded as a daring, graceful woman whose beauty, and other qualities, captivated Thomas Hardy; Harry Graham, a young playwright and poet best known for his *Ruthless Rhymes*; Anthony Hope, a barrister turned novelist and dramatist, famed for *The Prisoner of Zenda* which he wrote in just one month, and which was considered by many to be one of the finest romances ever published in the English language. Hope brought his young American wife, Elizabeth, with him and she was good company for fellow American, Ethel Barrymore – company, that is, while Harry Graham's presence was required on the field.

Players in the Allahakbarries also included a few good cricketers related to, or associated with, writer friends of Mr Barrie: Will Meredith, George Meredith's son; Charles Tennyson, Augustine Birrell's step-son; Thomas Gilmour, A. E. W. Mason's business manager. There were also two artists who worked within the literary world: Bernard Partridge, cartoonist for *Punch* magazine, and Henry J. Ford, best known for his illustrations of Andrew Lang's popular fairies books and, evidently, a 'real' cricketer.

But in 1905 Ford had agreed to play in the Artists team. This must have been a disappointment to Mr Barrie because in 1903 and 1904 his team had been soundly beaten by the Frensham Artists, a team championed by Mr Barrie's contemporaries, Allan James Hook and his younger brother, Bryan. They were two Kensington-born artist sons of the hugely successful and wealthy artist, James Clarke Hook, R.A. For many years, until his death in 1907, James Clarke Hook lived in Churt, then a village within the parish of Frensham, where he built and occupied a grand house called Silverdale. His two middle-aged sons and their large families also lived in the village. At that time, three other artists also lived in Frensham parish. Indeed, the area generally, seemingly an outpost of Kensington, was populated with more than its fair share of artists, writers and musicians. Evidently, the

Hooks had had no problem in attracting cricket players for their team, including some from farther afield: these included George Hillyard Swinstead, who lived at Islington; Henry Herbert La Thangue, from Chiswick; George Spencer Watson, from Kensington; and George Percy Jacomb-Hood from Fulham. It is possible, of course, that Mr Barrie may have helped in the initial assembly of the the Frensham Artists' team in order to secure another fixture for his all-important cricket week, for the Allahakbarries already had an annual fixture, each May, with another team of artists - a team led by the American, Edwin Abbey - and those matches were usually played in north Surrey, in places such as Denmark Hill and Esher, which were conveniently close to London.

Mr Barrie must have been most anxious that the Allahakbarries should win this third match at all costs, for he took some unprecedented steps. It was barely a year earlier that, almost as an afterthought, he had created the fictional character of Captain James Hook, an opponent for Peter Pan to overcome on stage. *Peter Pan* had opened in London to great acclaim a little over six months ago, and now it was the turn of the real James Hook to be defeated. So determined was Mr Barrie that the Allahakbarries should be successful in their 1905 match that he recruited not one, not two, but three 'really real' cricketers for the occasion. And so, for this match which, unlike the previous two at Frensham, was played in Farnham Park on July 3rd, former Kent County cricketer Frederic Meyrick-Jones, and former Middlesex County cricketers Edward Marsden and Sydney Pawling, were brought into Mr Barrie's team. As might be expected, their presence ensured a decisive victory: Allahakbarries: 257 for 5 declared, Meyrick-Jones 84, Marsden 76, Pawling 47. The Artists: 101 all out. Mr Barrie, who was ninth man and didn't get to bat, brought the match to an end when he caught the Artists' tenth man, Jacomb-Hood, off a ball from Marsden. For Mr Barrie, if not for his team mates, this must have been sweet revenge although, ironically, neither of the Hook brothers had selected themselves for the Artists' team for this final match. No matter. The noisy return of carloads of victorious cricketers and their ladies to the cottage was followed by a celebratory banquet and speeches in the garden, rounding off what was to prove the Allahakbarries' last cricket week. This must have been one of Mr Barrie's greatest moments of pleasure and satisfaction; he had defeated Hook's artists just as surely as Peter Pan had defeated Hook's pirates. Not surprisingly, we were left with more than the usual amount of clearing away once the last merry guests had left the cottage. With luck, I thought, breakfast the next morning might be required a little later than usual.

There was one other player in the Allahakbarries who I remember meeting in both 1904 and 1905, although he did not play in the final match against the Artists; I think he must have been displaced by one of the former county players. He was a journalist, two years younger than me, whose name didn't mean anything to me at the time. Many years later, when I read his novel *My Man Jeeves* and came across his sentence 'What with excellent browsing and sluicing and cheery conversation and what-not, the afternoon passed quite happily', I was immediately reminded by Pelham Grenville Wodehouse of the hectic cricket weeks at Black Lake Cottage and of the happiness they brought my former master.

Chapter 5

While the weather during first the week of July 1903 was gracious enough to allow the author his sporting indulgence, the rest of the month was very wet. And with the rain came the reign of peace, restored to the cottage and its garden following the departure of the Barries and their entourage of domestic staff and chauffeur a few days after the last guests had left for home. William and I then resumed possession of our respective territories, repaired any damage, and, with our equally hard-working assistants, started preparations for the next influx of visitors, which would begin in about three weeks' time.

Mr and Mrs Barrie always lived at Black Lake Cottage during the month of August. In some years the holiday would extend into part or all of September. When friends were not visiting, Mr Barrie would work in his upstairs room while his wife would immerse herself in her beautiful garden, caring for her floral offspring. At such times their dog, Luath, in 1903 still a young but already huge, shaggy black and white Newfoundland, was to be seen now standing at the open window opposite his master's door, now in his master's room, now sniffing his way round the garden, now with his mistress, now at the window again. Bounding in and out of the cottage, and up and down the narrow staircase, he was like an eager go-between who, alas, carried no messages of love or, indeed, messages of any sort, between the nine-years-married but still childless couple. It was not a good idea to be on the stairs at the wrong time, especially when carrying a tray up to the master.

On quiet days like those, Alice and I would serve lunch and tea for Mr and Mrs Barrie in one of their favourite spots in the garden. This was a secluded area at the lower end of the grassed orchard, between three large cherry trees and a tall privet hedge, on the west side of the cottage. The cherries offered dappled shade on hot sunny days, and the hedge screened the northerly, easterly and southerly winds. This sheltered spot, accessed through two archways in the four-foot thick hedge, was conveniently close to the back door and so we did not have far to fetch and carry everything. A handbell was used to announce that lunch or tea was being served. Sometimes this would succeed in fetching only Mrs Barrie for tea, the author preferring to remain in his room, working or writing letters. If his door was shut I was not to disturb him, for a writer usually wishes for no distractions, the more so when deadlines loom.

There were also other times when it was better not to seek out the author for anything so trivial as tea, nor even for lunch or dinner, for he often suffered from lengthy black moods and periods of depression. Mrs Barrie seemed to prefer, or maybe suffer, long periods of silence, too, for it was only when entertaining guests that she became lively in her husband's presence, perhaps putting on an act for their benefit. Witnessing such contrasts in behaviour, it was obvious to me that things were not right between the couple. But, of course, that was none of my business. They were my employers. They were in their forties, and married, whereas I was in my twenties, and single. What did I know?

Some years later I was saddened, but not very surprised, to read in my newspaper that James and Mary Barrie divorced in October 1909, about two years after Mary had fallen in love with a young writer named Gilbert Cannan. Mrs Barrie had managed to deceive her husband for most of that period but, eventually, her affair was revealed to Mr Barrie in July 1909 by their gardener at Black Lake Cottage, not William Cane but a successor. The gardener's wife had inadvertently discovered the adulterous nature of the relationship when taking cups of tea to the bedrooms early one morning in November 1908; she discovered that Cannan had spent the night with Mrs Barrie in her room. She and her husband kept their discovery a secret until the Mrs Barrie criticised the gardener's work, unjustly in his view. Tragic and scandalous as the whole business was, I was amazed at a strange coincidence: The name of the gardener who spilled the beans to Mr Barrie was Hunt, and his wife's name was Kate Hunt. Twenty years earlier at Black Lake Cottage, Henry Lewis's gardener was an elderly widower named George Hunt, and Lewis's cook was George Hunt's unmarried daughter, Kate Hunt!

It is easy to see that the Barries' marriage was doomed. The author was hopelessly romantic when it came to women. He would be struck by their beauty and fall in love with his imagined version of them, ignoring their actual qualities. I think this is what happened when he met and was immediately besotted with the pretty actress. The actress who, in turn, fell in love with him perhaps largely through admiration for his work, and then shaped herself to his ideas such that, superficially at least, she became his ideal woman. When she married him she ceased working as an actress and devoted herself to being a homemaker, a dutiful and proud wife and, perhaps most importantly, a beautiful hostess. All the while the former actress was happy living this way, the marriage probably seemed a happy one. But, eventually, she probably yearned to be loved for who she really was. Quite apart from the fact that while the marriage gave her no children – for, indeed, it was not consummated – and also the fact that her husband became infatuated with the attractive mother of another family, openly doting on her children, I think Mrs Barrie needed a different relationship. She needed one based on a full knowledge of one another's real characters, but she didn't get that relationship because Mr Barrie was a romanticist. In addition, the two had deceived each other from the outset, although they had done so in different ways: the author knew he was not temperamentally suited to married life, while, far less significantly, the actress knew she was six years older than she had led him to believe.

For years, Mr Barrie had suffered recurring nightmares in which he saw himself being dragged off unwillingly to be married in terrifying circumstances. This was on top of his knowledge that he lacked virility, a knowledge that had impelled him to shy away from approaching women as a red-blooded male. I think his mother had marked him in his impressionable years with her puritanical attitude towards sexual relations within marriage.

Mary Ansell, like many actresses anxious to remain in demand for as long as possible, had trimmed a few years off her age by stopping the clock for a period while she could get away with it. In those days, to do this was not unknown in certain circles, and a lady's age was not subject to public discussion. Lady Bracknell reminds us of this in Oscar Wilde's *The Importance of Being Earnest*: "Thirty-five is a very attractive age. London society is full of women of the very highest birth who have, of their own free choice, remained thiry-five for years." Mary Ansell made her free choice when ten years younger than this, and when, on the occasion of their marriage, she gave her age as twenty-seven she was, in fact, thirty-three, just ten months younger than her groom.

I wonder if Mr Barrie ever knew the truth. I think he was taken in for years by Mary's deception, possibly for the duration of their marriage, and that he may have discovered the truth only after some relevation or investigation late on. It is easy to reach this conclusion upon reading his one-act play *Rosalind* which made its first appearance on the London stage in 1912, just two years after his divorce from Mary. The play's leading characters were Charles, a young man in the springtime of his life who seems to have been largely based on George Davies, and Mrs Page, a middle-aged woman much based on Barrie's great friend, the actress Mrs Patrick Campbell. By some amazing piece of good fortune, Charles discovers he is in the house of the middle-aged mother of the one woman he loves. Or so it seems. Gradually, as Charles and Mrs Page, talk and compare photographs of the young Rosalind, Charles realises that all is not quite as he first thought. He begins to wonder if Mrs Page is in fact the girl who has stolen his heart, that the woman he loved was years older than she had led him to believe.

I think it is telling that Barrie included in this little play lines such as: "Dame, I don't know very much about the stage, but I do know that you should never, never ask an actress's age"; "There is nothing for them (ie. 'stars') between the ages of twenty-nine and sixty"; and "When you come to write my epitaph, Charles, let it be in these delicious words, 'She had a long twenty-nine'."

Of all the visits to Black Lake Cottage during August 1903, the strangest, for me, was from a man in his mid sixties who came down from his studio in Lambeth to draw sketches of the small front garden, the front of the cottage, and the hall and dining hall, and to make measurements and notes. His name was Walter Hann and he was a landscape artist, sculptor, and prolific theatrical scene designer and painter who had already painted scenes for several of Mr Barrie's plays and who, in another year's time, would be commissioned to produce some of the sets for *Peter Pan*. Hann had been asked to reproduce the large room as a set for *Little Mary* which was due to open in the West End at the end of September, starring Nina Boucicault. This wasn't the only time the cottage was used as the model for a set. In 1909, while on a visit to London, I went to see *What Every Woman Knows*, starring Gerald du Maurier and Hilda Trevelyan, and I was not entirely surprised to see the drawing room copied on stage, including a view into the garden beyond. Many years later I married my second husband, Arthur Hann but, as far as Arthur knew, he was not related to the scene painter.

As had occurred in the two previous summers, frequent visits to the cottage were made in 1903 by the Davies family, the family befriended by Mr Barrie after first meeting the two older boys, George and Jack, six years earlier in Kensington Gardens. Arthur and Sylvia Davies, whose home was not far from the Barries' house in Kensington, rented a cottage at Tilford. The cottage was only a mile down the road, and throughout most of August the Llewelyn Davieses, as they declared themselves to be, were constant companions of the Barries.

I liked the Davies family and I admired them for their public achievements and what they stood for. And now this polite and charming little branch had become drawn into the life and world of my master, and therefore I would have some contact with the family. But, because I was a Llewellyn, I found it slightly irritating that Sylvia insisted on being called Mrs Llewelyn Davies when I believed that her husband's surname was merely

Davies. Doubtless Arthur had Llewelyns, or Llewellyns, somewhere in his ancestry but, surely, in this world of theirs, and mine, where everything had to be right and proper, his wife was either Sylvia Davies or, formally, Mrs Arthur Llewelyn Davies. I had been brought up to understand that it was fairly common practice for Welsh Llewelyns and Llewellyns, and their descendants, to bestow on their offspring the forename version, spelt 'Llewelyn', but that by doing this there was no intention to create compound surnames.

Before marriage, Sylvia had enjoyed the rather grand name of Sylvia Jocelyn Busson du Maurier, daughter of a man with an even bigger mouthful, the Paris born author and artist George Louis Palmella Busson du Maurier, and sister of the actor Gerald du Maurier. Gerald, incidentally, later fathered the famous author Daphne du Maurier who was born in 1907. George du Maurier began life in France as plain George Maurier and he prefixed his surname with 'du' as an affectation while still a young man. Maybe taking such liberties with names was peculiar to a certain class of people determined to set themselves apart in one way, if not in another. It occurred to me that, had I been in a similar position to George Maurier, an aspiring writer desirous of creating a unique and memorable name for myself, I might have had the gall to choose the nom de plume of Sue de Nimes. But I digress.

Faced with relinquishing her pseudo-aristocratic maiden name, had Sylvia considered that her married name of Sylvia Davies would be insufficiently imposing? Had she persuaded her future husband to create a double-barrelled surname for himself which Sylvia could then use in deference to her mother's opinion on the matter, wherein appearances and impressions would seem to have been of paramount importance? Sylvia's mother had shown reservations about her daughter marrying Arthur because of his relative lack of money, and the two families had been worlds apart in their way of life. Arthur was a barrister who practised as Arthur Llewelyn Davies. Llewelyn was merely his second forename, however, as indeed it was also merely his father John's second forename. Both father and son were educated at Cambridge University, father as Davies, John L., and son as Davies, Arthur L. When John Llewelyn Davies married Mary Crompton his wife became Mrs Mary Davies, for Davies was her surname as stated by her husband on at least two formal occasions; the name Llewelyn did not attach to her.

Perhaps my problem with this originated with all six of John's sons being given Llewelyn as their second forename, and then John choosing, part-way through his life, to sign his name, in my view misleadingly, as 'J. Llewelyn Davies'. It was therefore a straightforward matter for each of his sons to choose whether to follow suit and encourage people to regard his name whichever way he preferred.

The Reverend John Llewelyn Davies was a man I admired greatly for being a supporter of workers' rights and women's suffrage. He understood the lot of the common worker and that of women in their own right. He had achieved many great things and had been Chaplain to Queen Victoria and, indeed, was now Chaplain to the King. He had not passed on his middle name to all his children, however. His first-born, Margaret, who was secretary to the Women's Co-operative Guild, and was a leading feminist along with Clementina Black, Clara Collet, Elizabeth Garrett Anderson and the Pankhursts, became well-known as Margaret Llewelyn Davies, but John and his wife had actually named her Margaret Caroline Davies, Caroline being her maternal grandmother's first name. Perhaps Margaret Davies adopted Llewelyn as a middle name so as to be publically associated with her respected father, for they were fighting for the same cause.

One thing was certain in all this: John Llewelyn Davies had not inherited a compound surname. His brother William's full name was William Stephen Davies, and that of his sister was Sarah Emily Davies, the same (Sarah) Emily Davies who, with Barbara Bodichon, organised the first women's suffrage petition to Parliament in 1866, and who was the principal founder of the College for Women at Benslow House, Hitchin, in 1869; within four years the College was renamed Girton College and removed to new buildings at Cambridge, and Emily directed the College's financial and general policy until 1904. In 1948 Girton received the status of a College of Cambridge University.

It was as a matter of principle, as well as admitted obstinacy on my part, that I would insist on referring to everyone in John's family as simply the Davieses. To me it was simply the truth.

The weather in August 1903 was generally cool, very wet and windy at times, and there were even gales in the middle of the month. Consequently, much of the time was spent indoors and various games and entertainments were arranged to keep the Davies boys occupied and amused. I recall that several versions of games of marbles were favoured by Mr Barrie; Alice was forever picking up stray marbles found in odd corners and under furniture. But, whenever possible, there were outdoor activities and walks, bicycle rides, visits to other friends, and excursions in the car, for the Lanchester was still very much a novelty for the older boys: George aged ten, Jack who was nearly nine, and Peter aged six.

The car seemed even more of a novelty to Luath who, as we noticed from the long kitchen window which overlooked the drive, was always the first passenger to jump on to the car. In doing this, however, he hardly lived up to the meaning of his name. Luath, as Mr Barrie once told me, is Gaelic for swift or nimble. Luath succeeded in being first on to the car more by being large, strong and, to put it politely, enthusiastic. For some reason, if only the matching colouring, Mr Barrie named Porthos's successor after the ploughman's black and white collie in the poem *The Twa Dogs* by Robert Burns. In that poem Burns had immortalised his own little collie, a favourite dog who had been killed while wandering away from his master. Luath is an unusual name. I wonder if Mr Barrie had also considered the other Luath in literature, one I discovered many years later: one of Cuthullin's hunting dogs in Ossian's *Fingal*, wherein Cuthullin's Luath was described as having 'surly strength'. Whatever the truth, true to form Mr Barrie marked his Luath's existence in one of his works; he used his coat as the model for Nana's in *Peter Pan*.

The Lanchester was viewed by the domestic staff as an incredible luxury, costing more to own and run than the employment of several of the likes of us, but, of course, the Barries could easily afford the vehicle and its driver. I thought Fred had a glamourous occupation, transporting famous people all over the place, especially in London, picking them up and dropping them off at posh establishments. His passengers placed their lives in his hands as he raced along at up to twenty miles per hour, and maybe even at a reckless thirty miles per hour. Fred saw it differently, however, and reminded me that those same people placed their lives in my hands when they dined at Black Lake Cottage. Blooming cheek!

For Fred there were long periods – hours, sometimes days – when he was not required to drive the car. During those times, having ensured daily the serviceability and cleanliness of the vehicle, he was expected to run errands and busy himself with handyman type jobs around the place. I liked that because it meant that I got to see more of him, and on some Sundays he was permitted to drive the servants to church. Sometimes he would drive me into Farnham on shopping errands, for Mrs Barrie often decided she needed one thing or another in a hurry. She rarely journeyed into Farnham for shopping purposes herself, however, and I didn't mind that one bit.

Mr Barrie loved creating adventures for the boys and himself. These were enacted in the garden and the surrounding woods, including in and around Black Lake which was hidden from view beyond the the pine trees opposite the cottage. Mr Barrie was devoted to the boys and would sometimes play with them all day.

On one very special day in my life I was privileged to be invited to join in one of these adventures but I have to admit that, at the time, I thought it was rather silly. Mind you, I knew better than to say as much to Mr Barrie. I had already learnt that it was safest to take him seriously at all times. He could be very persuasive when he wanted something. He insisted that I leave my work to join in a bear hunt in the sloping pine woods just beyond the garden behind the cottage. His games were enactments of scenes he had already created in his mind and evidently there was a part for me in this one.

We had to crawl on hands and knees on the mercifully soft carpet of pine needles and moss, underlain with peat, carrying imaginary guns and stalking our own tame white rabbits who ran before us and represented the bears. Pine tree trunks, and the occasional low clump of bilberry bushes, afforded sparse cover for the daring hunters, especially for me as I was easily the largest. It was therefore entirely logical to my companions, particularly our leader who, as always, hunted dressed in a three-piece suit, polished lace-up shoes or boots, and a crumpled hat, and with pipe in mouth, and notebook, pencil, tobacco pouch, matches and goodness knows what else in bulging pockets - that I, and not he in his inappropriate camouflage, should be the one to be spotted by the bears. I protested mildly that bears were short-sighted and that they would have to scent me but it was to no avail, for I was reminded that we had been careful to keep downwind of our quarry. Obediently supine, I resigned myself to being mauled and trampled by one of the vicious beasts. For some reason, however, neither of the rabbits was willing to imitate the action of the bear. I think they were pre-occupied with finding something far more interesting, such as a few blades of grass. And so it was not only an imaginary brute but an invisible one that had to attack me, thus enabling my friends to conclude the dramatist's carefully planned scene by gallantly saving my life at the last possible moment.

The giant Luath was present throughout our adventure and I was fearful for the rabbits' safety, afraid that he might suddenly take the adventure too seriously, but, rather than pounce on the rabbits, or indeed on me, he spent most of the time alternately barking and staring, seemingly in disbelief at the unique spectacle. Well, he was still young and had a lot to learn. It was good to know that his master was educating him in all aspects of normal human behaviour.

After some sort of victory dance, the smaller two of my heroes carried the pair of petrified pets back down to the safety and comfort of their familiar run among the apple and pear trees of the orchard. Then, as a reward for my rescue, I invited the hunters into the unexplored territory that was my kitchen, for clandestine cakes and fruit jellies. As may be imagined, the first to finish his jelly was Luath who then disappeared once more into the garden only to return a minute later carrying a hedgehog, quite unharmed, in his mouth. Thank you, Luath, not for the prickly gift, fleas and all, but for giving me a rare opportunity to see my master smile.

We now know, of course, that games such as this were providing the author with ideas and inspiration for parts of his play, *Peter Pan*, although the character of Peter Pan had already appeared within *The Little White Bird*. The Davies boys were being used by Mr Barrie, if only through observation, to note occurrences, actions, reactions and comments, and it all seemed to me to be innocent, harmless fun. Mr Barrie made no secret of what he was doing, and occasionally he could be seen jotting down notes lest he should forget some detail, or thought, which might have its use later, sometimes much later. Interestingly, he wrote with his right hand, yet I had noticed that in many things he was left handed. In his youth, he had been made to write with his right hand. Years later, however, he switched to writing with his left hand, evidently with little difficulty, following a bout of writer's cramp.

The Davies boys were by no means the only unwitting providers of ideas for the author. Alice Lamport was another. I believe that her experiences gave Mr Barrie some of the inspiration for his play, *Alice Sit-by-the-Fire*, which he wrote in 1903, revising it in 1904. Consider this: In 1897, Alice Lamport gave birth to a girl which she named Isabel. The young father, Henry James Kinge, never saw the baby because he was in the army and, during Alice's pregnancy, was posted to India for eight years. Alice needed to keep working and found it difficult to cope with her baby at the same time, so Henry's parents brought up Isabel at their home in West Street, Farnham. They did this until their son had served his term and returned home to be united with his daughter and to marry Alice. In the play, Alice Grey is the wife of an Army colonel who had been posted to

India for five years. She had gone with him and, while there, had had a baby girl. When the baby was aged two months it was sent back to England where it was nursed for seventeen months before its parents returned. Just as in the real life situation, therefore, Alice Grey and her husband then had the problem of re-adapting themselves to their baby. In addition, the housemaid's name in the play is Fanny, and Fanny Lamport had been the other housemaid at Black Lake Cottage. In the spring of 1905, Henry Kinge returned to England. At about the same time, the play opened in London's West End with Ellen Terry in the title role. In the summer, three months later, Henry married Alice Lamport and *Alice Sit-by-the-Fire* completed its short run.

Alice finished working at Black Lake Cottage when she married Henry but her story does not quite end there. Her husband found employment with Farnham Rural District Council as an assistant sanitary inspector for the Hindhead area. In 1906, another girl, Myrtle Joyce, was added to the family and, in 1909, Alice started what rapidly became a highly successful, very select bed and breakfast establishment at Hindhead. Her many satisfied guests were soon to include Baroness Orcxy, who wrote *The Scarlet Pimpernel*, and Lady Lloyd George. Quite amazing when you consider that Alice's father was an agricultural labourer and Henry's father a brewery labourer. I shouldn't be surprised if Mr and Mrs Barrie helped her get started, or, at the very least, recommended her place to their many friends. Mr Barrie was known for many acts of kindness and generosity, and I daresay there were many other instances which were not revealed. In later years, Peter Scott used to visit a long-stay guest at Alice's house and, during the second world war, the house was a safe house for the wife of the Polish president Wladyslaw Raczkiewicz.

I knew of two more instances of Mr Barrie basing fictional characters or situations on real people and events. Several years after I finished working for him, I thought I recognised something of myself, and not merely my name, in the character of Mabel Purdie in *Dear Brutus*. In that play I saw Barrie as Lob, and the setting as Black Lake Cottage, situated, as indeed it was, in the enchanted woods. Enchanted woods of pine trees planted in about 1860, the year of Barrie's birth - now there was a coincidence. The enchanted woods also of George Meredith's poem *The Woods of Westermain*? - 'Enter these enchanted woods, you who dare' - Who is to say? The term came into Barrie's head somehow. Writers borrowed phrases unashamedly and flatteringly from others, and Barrie often wrote short notes and observations about people, and the things they said, or ideas which sprang from those, for possible use sooner or later.

Sometimes Barrie used the same groups of names for his fictional characters as existed in real life. He also used the Christian names of family and friends. In *What Every Woman Knows*, the main character, Maggie Wylie, has two brothers, David and James. In life, James Barrie had a younger sister named Maggie and an older brother named David. Maggie would be my next employer. David, however, died on the day before his fourteenth birthday.

David Barrie died in an accident in Kirriemuir in January 1867. While his friend donned a pair of skates, David walked on to the ice in his shoes. Somehow his skating friend collided with him and David was knocked off his feet. He fell and fractured his skull on the ice. Curiously, Barrie's father, also named David, also died after being knocked off his feet, in his case by a horse and cart. But he was eighty-seven and had lived a full term of life.

David was everything that James was not, and the apple of his mother's eye. The consequences of his sudden death, in particular the sad and distressing behaviour of his mother during her protracted grieving, had a profound and permanent effect on James Barrie. Looked at objectively, she was inconsiderate towards the emotional needs and innocent feelings of her youngest son, then aged five, who tried everything he could think of to console her but failed. The whole experience shaped his mind in his formative years with consequent effect on his life. James might not have become a writer were it not for that accident, but even if we assume that he would still have made his living through his pen the world might not have been given Peter Pan. While there was no escaping the fact that David had been prevented from growing up, James might not have had to mature so fast, missing out on a full childhood, and so might not have had the inspiration to create the boy who couldn't grow up.

When I discovered *Dear Brutus* I found it intriguing to ponder whether, if Barrie had been given the opportunity to change his life from some point in his past, as he had given his characters in the play, he would have restrained his brother from walking on to the ice to watch his friend on that fateful day. And did Barrie himself ever ponder that, and be lead to the obvious consequence that he might not have become the huge success that he was, but he might have known great personal happiness? I feel sure he did. While he believed that people would make the same mistakes, his 'second chance' theme fascinated him yet possibly dogged him all his life.

Alternatively, he might have reasoned that, because he was only five and short for his age, while his brother was almost fourteen and tall with it, he would not have been physically capable of restraining him, in which case David would have died anyway. This might have led him to wonder whether, if he had managed to come up with just one more approach towards his inconsolable mother, he might have succeeded in changing his mother's behaviour toward him.

Back to the summer of 1903. Young Michael Davies was only three years old and therefore too young for bear hunting and some of the other outdoor games and adventures enjoyed by his brothers with their 'Uncle Jim'. His turn would come, as would that of the fifth boy, Nico, with whom Mrs Davies was six months pregnant. I didn't see Nico until June 1905 when Mrs Davies brought him and Michael to stay for a holiday. That was during the time when the Lucases and the Hewletts also stayed at the cottage. On that occasion Michael got to play with a bear of his own - quite a large brown one, on wheels, and on which he would ride, pulled along by Edward Verrall Lucas's daughter, Audrey, and also by his mother and his doting 'uncle'.

For now, Michael and Nico were kept amused for much of the time by their nurse, Mary Hodgson, and her assistant nurse, Anna Spring, a Swiss-born girl of twenty-one. The Davies's other domestic staff, Eliza Webb and Elizabeth Harper, both cooks, and Eleanor Dawson, housemaid, also appeared at Black Lake Cottage. It was always interesting to meet such people and compare notes, and kitchen gossip was a useful way of learning more about our respective employers, their families and friends, and something of what they all got up to. But it behove us to keep such information just between ourselves, and never to be caught whispering or in a huddle. I found that Elizabeth and Eleanor, together with Mary Hodgson, were all born in Kirkby Lonsdale, Westmorland, where the Reverend John L. Davies was rector, and that Arthur Davies had actively sought his domestic staff from among families known to him or his family. Mary Hodgson's father was a stonemason who had died while Mary was still a child, and she had previously been employed as a young nurse by Arthur's brother, Maurice. Eleanor's father also was a stonemason, and born in the same village as Mary's father, while Elizabeth's father was a farmer.

Despite my unease at what I felt was misuse of the Llewelyn name by Mrs Davies, there was no question that the members of the Davies family were delightful, high-achieving people, and I respected them enormously. During my time with the Barries the young boys, too, were adorable and always well-mannered towards everyone, including me. Sadly, shortly after I moved on to my next position, the family began to suffer tragedy upon tragedy, each one reported in the newspapers, and time and again my heart went out to them, and to Mr Barrie to whom I knew they all meant so much. 'The Five' lost their father in 1907 and their mother in 1910, both of whom succumbed to cancer before reaching the age of forty-five. Mr Barrie then became the boys' guardian and surrogate father. Thereafter, George was killed at Flanders in the First World War in 1915 when aged twenty-one, and Michael drowned in a notoriously dangerous section of the Thames near Sandford bathing pool, Oxford, in 1921 when aged twenty – he was found with a male friend, Rupert Buxton, their hands clasped together, apparently the result of either a double suicide pact or an attempt by one of them to rescue the other. The inquest resulted in a verdict of accidental drowning. Of the five brothers, I think George and Michael were the closest to Mr Barrie's heart. Years after Mr Barrie's death, Jack and Peter died in their early sixties, Peter committing suicide in 1960 by throwing himself in front of a London Underground train at Sloane Square station.

Despite their being at least fourteen years my junior, I outlived all of the boys except Nico. Now and then, in the press, I read of suggestions that Mr Barrie had been, shall we say, a questionable influence on the lives of the Davies family, especially the boys. I believe such insinuations were groundless. I think that while his various attentions may have had some inadvertent consequences his intentions were always honourable. D. H. Lawrence encapsulated my feelings when, upon learning of Michael Davies's death, he wrote, in a letter to Mary Cannan dated July 4th 1921, 'J. M. (Barrie) has a fatal touch for those he loves'.

Mabel Bessie LLewellyn, about 1903.

Mary Ansell in 1891.

Mary Ansell, about 1894.

J. M. Barrie in about 1903.

J. M. Barrie with Luath in 1904.

*Alice Kinge (née Lamport) and her
second daughter Myrtle Joyce Kinge, 1906.*

Archibald Ellis Jones and Mabel, 1915.

Mabel with Robert Greenham and Billy, 1947.

Chapter 6

Now, up again in roar and wrath
High soaring and wide sweeping; now,
With sudden fury dashing down
Full-force on the awaiting woods.

From *South-West Wind in the Woodland* by George Meredith

The Barries' summer holiday of 1903 came to an end at the beginning of September, just as the weather improved dramatically. Overall, it had been a poor summer but now it was extremely hot for a few days and, with the chauffeur-driven departure of Mr and Mrs Barrie and Luath, there came a return to quiet days and free access to the whole cottage and garden. I treated myself to the luxury of some carefree relaxation walking and cycling in the countryside around Tilford and Frensham and, of course, strolling in the shade of the pines and Mr Barrie's 'haunted groves of Waverley' where I found that my roaming thoughts sometimes alighted on Fred. I had taken a shine to him but, so far, he hadn't given any indication that he was attracted to me. Perhaps he never would.

The heatwave proved to be short-lived, a lull before the storm if ever there was one. On the tenth of September severe gales swept across England bringing down many trees and blocking roads and paths. For hours the high wind roared through the pines surrounding Black Lake Cottage and its frightened occupant. George Meredith would have loved it here, and I would have appreciated his company. Then temperatures dropped sharply. As if that wasn't enough, the next month was extremely wet. According to a newspaper report, that October was the wettest month of all in England and Wales since records began in 1766. There was much flooding, and there were gales and storms; tornadoes hit Wareham and Banbury. Bridges were weakened and many of them collapsed. Travel was severely disrupted. Little wonder, then, that the Barries chose not to visit their cottage for some time, and I began to realise that opportunities to see Fred were going to be few and far between for quite some time.

In complete contrast, November was uneventful weatherwise, but there were two significant events in Mr Barrie's life. On November 24th Sylvia Davies gave birth to her fifth and last child, Nicholas, who soon became known as Nico. But, far more importantly, not only for Mr Barrie but for the world, on November 23rd the author started work on *Anon. A Play*. He had a problem settling on a good title, however. Three months later he would refer to it as *Peter and Wendy*. Wendy? Who or what was Wendy? Two months after that, when obliged to give it a title for presentation to Charles Frohman, Barrie would name it *The Great White Father*. Frohman liked the play but not the title. He would suggest it be called *Peter Pan* and Barrie would accede to that.

Peter Pan was the play that would introduce to the world the invented name of Wendy, and the children's Wendy house. The origin of Wendy lay in the early 1890s when the young daughter of poet and playwright W. E. Henley and wife Hannah had addressed Barrie as 'my friendy'. Margaret Emma Henley did this because her father referred to Barrie as 'my friend', but she had difficulty with enunciating some letters, in particular the letter 'r'. Thus, in copying her father, 'my friendy' had sounded like 'my fwendy', and she had called Barrie her 'fwendy-wendy'. At some point Barrie decided to establish and immortalise the name of Wendy, and it seems that he reached his decision in late 1903.

What prompted Barrie to do this when Margaret had died almost ten years previously? Twenty-three days after tubercular meningitis was diagnosed, little Margaret died on February 11th 1894 when aged just five years and five months. Not long after that sad event Barrie had been moved to give her a brief appearance in his novel *Sentimental Tommy*; she was Reddy, a childhood frend of Tommy's who dies at the age of six. Barrie had marked the ginger-haired Margaret's passing seemingly without any thought of Wendy. Or, if the idea of creating the new name had occurred to him at that time, so soon after Margaret's death, he had presumably resisted the temptation out of consideration for the feelings of her parents and kept the idea for possible future use.

I think Barrie's decision to create the name of Wendy may not have come about had it not been for the death of Margaret's father, in Surrey, in July 1903. Henley's death probably affected Barrie deeply, for he had indeed been Barrie's friend. He was a Gloucester-born man who, in his boyhood, had contracted tuberculosis and become crippled and, in 1873, had had his lower left leg amputated. He had spent twenty months recuperating in Edinburgh Infirmary and thereafter used a wooden leg. In 1878 he married a Scottish girl, Hannah Johnson Boyle, in Midlothian. While in Edinburgh, Henley became friendly with another sufferer from tuberculosis, Robert Louis Stevenson, with whom he collaborated on four plays in the early 1880s. It was Henley who gave Stevenson the inspiration for his peg-legged character Long John Silver in *Treasure Island*. By the late 1880s Henley had published some of Barrie's early writings in the *National Observer*, and Stevenson, Barrie's hero, had gone to live in the South Pacific, from where he conducted a lengthy correspondence with Barrie until his death in Samoa in 1894. Henley's death must have evoked memories, including ones of Margaret and 'fwendy-wendy', and, in Barrie's mind, it probably closed an episode: an episode which he could preserve through the creation of Wendy. And to Wendy he added a poignant touch: for the first production of *Peter Pan*, he ordered that Margaret's favourite cloak be copied, from a portrait, for use as part of Wendy's costume.

Also in November, and of absolutely no importance to the world, it became abundantly clear to me that I would be underemployed at Black Lake Cottage during the colder months of the year, for I learned that, yet again, the Barries did not intend to spend Christmas away from their London home. This really was a summer cottage. Consequently I reported my concerns to Mr and Mrs Barrie and, in December, after some deliberation, a change in my employment was agreed. From January 1904, I was to live mainly at the home of Mr and Mrs Winter, at Medstead, Hampshire, and to work for them as housekeeper at all times other than when I would be required to be at Black Lake Cottage for the busy social occasions there. In the meantime, as the Barries saw no need for me to linger at the cottage, I was given permission to get packed as soon as I wished and to have a Christmas holiday. There would be no break in my pay, which was a relief. As had happened the previous winter, Alice would continue as housemaid, visiting the cottage as necessary to keep things dusted and polished, and to redirect any letters and cards which William Annals, the Tilford postman, might deliver. During the week before Christmas, therefore, I made my preparations for my flight from Black Lake Cottage, all the while quite unaware that, in his study at Leinster Corner, James Barrie was thinking about making his characters fly above the stage, and, in Kitty Hawk, North Carolina, two brothers named Wilbur and Orville Wright were about to wow the world with the news that they had finally achieved sustained powered flight in their wonderful wood-and-fabric biplane.

Chapter 7

I decided to spend Christmas at Mayflower with my parents and as many of my brothers and sisters as would be there. It was many months since I had seen any of them. As Medstead lay on the railway line between Farnham and Poole I arranged to break my journey there to deposit my trunk at The Boynes, and I would take just my suitcase the rest of the way. The bicycle would remain available for use at the cottage.

The pale mid-December day of my leaving Black Lake Cottage was cold and windy, and I was glad of the shelter of the waiting room at Farnham Station. I walked over to one of the windows on either side of the stove and looked out over the station yard. From here I saw that any view of Tilford Road, whence I had just come, was obscured by a large goods shed on the far side of the yard. It was as if this drab, depressing building was intent on blocking all memory of the Barries and their guests, and of Fred, whom I had not seen for over three months. But I comforted myself with the thought that I would be seeing them again in the spring.

For most of the distance to Medstead the train ran alongside the meandering upper reaches of the Alton branch of the River Wey, the same river which, downstream, flows past Black Lake and under Tilford Bridge. The river's several tributary sources include two at Chawton, where Jane Austin had lived the last few years of her life. I was to ride on this slow line several times over the next two years, and it became known to me affectionately as the Railwey Line. It became known to others as the Watercress Line, however, because it was useful in carrying large quantities of watercress from Alresford, south to Winchester and Southampton, and north to London.

Not long out of Alton, the train slowed and the engine had to work harder, chuff-chuffing up the slightly snaking incline leading to the single-track line's hilltop, where it passed through a narrow, high, vertical sided chalk cutting before arriving suddenly at Medstead station where, as at all the stations on this section of the line, the track divided into two so as to allow trains to pass each other. This station, I discovered later, was the highest in southern England. I alighted hoping for some help with my luggage. Mr Winter had said not to worry about needing any transport as his house was only a couple of hundred yards from the station. That was all very well but I couldn't carry my trunk anywhere. Fortunately, just as the train was pulling out of the station, help arrived.

"Would you like some help with your trunk, miss?"

"Yes, please. I'm looking for The Boynes which is supposed to be close by, but I can't see it."

"That's because it's hidden behind those trees, over the other side of the station. 'Tis only a bungalow, d'you see. You just wait here while I fetch the barrow and I'll wheel your luggage over there. We'll need to go across the line at the end of the platform."

Charlie Durrant, born in Farnham and the son of a painter, had been the stationmaster at Medstead for almost two years, and you couldn't wish for a more helpful railway man. He lived with his wife and three young children in the house beside the station, and I was to get to know all of them quite well. Aged thirty-six, Charlie had moved there from Alton where he had been head clerk at the town's railway station. He had met his wife, Ada, when she was a schoolteacher living at Ropley, a village with the next station down the line from Medstead. Ada was five years his senior and hailed originally from Islington.

Talking non-stop all the way, and rejecting an offer of help from one of the two young look-alike porters, William and Frederick Holland, Charlie took my luggage out of the station, along the first part of a narrow, stony lane and into a drive, right to the front door of the double-fronted, white painted bungalow that was the centrepiece of The Boynes. Such service for a stranger, I thought, but then this seemed to be a quiet station, and I was a pretty, young woman of twenty-four ...

"Thank you, Charlie, that was very kind of you."

"Think nothing of it, Miss. I've done the same for Mr Barrie when he's visited his sister, although, come to think of it, it must be over a year since I saw him last. We've always looked after the Barries here. Charlie Pfrangley, the stationmaster who was here before me, he started it years ago and it became custom and practice, as you might say. It would seem rude if we stopped now. Anyway, Ada and I, we're the closest neighbours of the Winters. What's a neighbour for if he can't lend a hand now and then? I hope you enjoy your stay."

"Oh, I'm not staying. Well, not until after Christmas. I'll be catching the next train on to Southampton, and then to Poole to visit my parents."

At this, Charlie looked a little puzzled.

"Then why didn't you stay on your train just now? I could have fetched your trunk over here and saved you the wait."

"That's kind of you," I said, "but I never expected such help would be available. I wanted to meet Mrs Winter and take a look at my new home and workplace."

"Then you'll be taking your suitcase on to Poole. Let me take it back now and you can collect it from my office. It'll be quite safe with me. The next train's at ten past eleven." And with that, the cheerful Charlie charged off with his barrow, and I turned and knocked on the door, looking forward to getting out of the cold and, hopefully, sipping a warming cup of tea.

The Christmas season with my family was enjoyed, and endured, and the day after New Year's Day, 1904, saw me back at The Boynes for the start of the next phase of my life as a housekeeper. My transfer from Black Lake Cottage suited the Winters because their son, William, who was called Willie so as not to be confused with his father, had reached the age of six, and the nurse, Elsie Duke, had not long departed. The only other servant in the household was Flora Herrington, a thirty year old dairyman's daughter originally from Norton Ferris in far west Wiltshire but whose father had moved his family around a lot in the Bruton Forest and Cranborne Chase areas, largely in the vicinity of the Stourhead and Longleat estates. Just as had happened with Alice at Black Lake Cottage, Flora was pleased at my arrival for she also had been trying recently to cope with all the domestic work herself. It soon became clear to me that the Barries hadn't transferred me to the Winters' home merely to honour the one year contract between us, and I could see that I was going to have my work cut out to satisfy the requirements of both households, especially in the spring and summer.

Mrs Margaret Winter, known to family and friends as Maggie, was Barrie's younger sister and she doted on her famous brother to whom she had been especially close all her life. She sang his praises to everyone: servants, family, friends and visitors. He could do no wrong. In the few years before marrying William in 1893, she had spent much time staying with her brother at his several London lodgings which included the house of Miss Christine Rae at 15 Old Cavendish Street. Mrs Winter told me she and William had found their Medstead home shortly before their marriage when they visited this part of east Hampshire partly at William's suggestion but also because she recalled a recommendation to do so by Alice Fitt, one of Miss Rae's two servants, who was born at nearby Selborne and who had frequently enthused about the countryside there and the ease of access from London by railway. But Mrs Winter would not have been there at all, nor would she have been married to William, had it not been for a tragic incident which had occurred in Scotland. She had been engaged to William's younger brother, the Reverend James Winter, a friend of the Barrie family, but James had been killed when flung from his horse just three weeks before he and Maggie were to be married. The horse had been an early wedding gift from James Barrie, and it was to enable James Winter to get around his rural parish more easily. Mr Barrie became overcome by guilt, feeling that he was to blame for the death of his future brother-in-law and, as a consequence of this, he vowed to care for his sister ever after.

In 1882 William Winter had graduated from Clare College, Cambridge, a 26th Wrangler, and now he used his knowledge and experience to coach young men in mathematics, at Medstead, to prepare them for entrance to university. I found him to be a real gentleman; his warm and courteous manner at my interview had been entirely in character and not adopted for the occasion. He was a consistently quiet and kind man who seemed throughly organised and professional, and I observed that he was a considerate, loving husband to Mrs Winter and a model father to their son.

In my view, young Willie Winter was over-indulged by his parents, but then his mother seemed always to have time on her hands. He was a very active and bright boy but, unlike his father, terribly untidy. What a contrast there was between this one child family and my own large family and the families of my relatives. Later, preferring to be known as William, not Willie, he made his mark as a teenager when he won the City of London Chess Club championship shortly before entering Clare College, Cambridge, to study Law. In adulthood, he went on to become British Men's Chess Champion in 1935 and 1936 and, while not achieving World Champion status, he nevertheless beat a number of the world's top players. He was one of the more colourful characters in the game and became the chess correspondent for the *Manchester Guardian* and the *Daily Worker*. He also wrote two acclaimed books: *Chess for Match Players* and *Kings of Chess*, the latter just a year before his death at the age of 57. Chess was not his only strong point for, though disorganised, William was a man of many talents and he was utterly serious about politics. Between the two world wars he was an active public speaker for the Communist Party and was so successful at stirring up public feeling that at one stage he was found guilty of sedition and had to serve a six-month prison sentence.

I was never sure of the depth of the relationship between the young Willie and his 'Uncle Jim'. While Mr Barrie paid visits to The Boynes and spent time with his nephew, it seemed to me that he was not as close to Willie as I had seen he was to the Davies boys. Certainly the only evidence hanging on the walls lay in two sepia photographs taken just outside the front of the house. One was of Willie, the other of Mr Barrie, and I supposed that each had been photographed by the other. I never thought to ask.

During my time there Mr Barrie's visits to his sister's home were infrequent and became less so, and they were of short duration, a few hours at most. But it had not always been thus, for one of the first things Mrs Winter had proudly showed me upon my arrival was the study which she had had constructed specially for her brother's use. Mr Barrie had been a frequent visitor during the early years of their marriage, usually staying for extended periods and taking advantage of the peace and quiet, away from London, to progress his writing. He had worked on his *Sentimental Tommy* during a protracted stay here in the autumn of 1893 for, at that time, while he had met and fallen in love with Mary Ansell over a year earlier, Mr Barrie was still unmarried and had no permanent home. The author married the actress on July 9th 1894 and he worked further on *Sentimental Tommy* during another stay, this time with his wife present, in the autumn of that year. After a few weeks lodging at Fowey, Cornwall, the couple returned to The Boynes for Christmas. Evidently, Mrs Winter had envisaged her brother making extensive use of her home for some years, regardless of his marriage and where that might take him.

The Boynes was essentially a rectangular bungalow with a skylighted central passage starting from the square entrance hall and running most of its length to a smaller hall. The small kitchen was at the far left hand end, leading off the second hall, and the study was the upper floor of a modest two storey extension which had been built on to that corner. It was accessible only from the kitchen via a nondescript door which concealed a flight of fourteen narrow, steep stairs, and thus was shielded from the main household. A discrete room discreetly placed. Part way up the stairs there was a low cross-beam, so low that even Mr Barrie had to be careful not to bang his head on it. The study's only window faced a little east of south, letting in the sunshine for the morning and much of the afternoon and affording a fairly narrow but commanding view of a small garden to the side of the bungalow, the garden where the washing was hung out to dry. With the writing desk placed at the window, the author could see, to the left, the roofs of the bungalow and, in the middle distance ahead, several trees. To the right were a few trees and a field beyond, and, beyond the field, the railway embankment. Through the trees, he could see the clouds of smoke rising from locomotives as they strained to haul their trains up the long, steep gradient from the Alresford and Winchester direction, 'over the Alps', on the railway line which connected him conveniently to Waterloo and his life in the capital.

During my time at The Boynes the study was hardly used by Mr Barrie, yet it was determinedly maintained as such by his hero-worshipping sister. If it had ever been adequately equipped for brief periods of research, it certainly was not now, for the shelves supported few books. From 1900, with the author having not only his main study at his London home at Leinster Corner, but also a desk at Black Lake Cottage, this room represented nothing more than a temporary retreat, a bolt hole for the writing of notes or an occasional letter, and then only on the rare occasions when the author was visiting his sister. Whenever I looked back on 1904, it always saddened me that the original script for *Peter Pan*, the most famous and enduring of Barrie's works, which saw its first performance in at the Duke of York's Theatre in London on December 27th 1904, was not written in the room adjoining my kitchen. On the other hand, it tickled me to know that I had known its author at the time, and that The Boynes had at least made one contribution to *Peter Pan*: According to Mrs Winter the elaborate ceiling lamp in the hall, one of several lamps which I had to light each evening, had given Barrie the inspiration for how Tinkerbell would be made to appear on stage. The lamp was a lantern suspended from a ceiling hook by a system of three chains with pulleys so that when the oil reservoir was pulled downwards the six-sided, coloured glass shade rose by the same distance. When the wick was lit, a point of white light appeared and grew in intensity, the twinkling point of light of the dying fairy. Then, as the light was raised the shade lowered around it, casting a moving pattern of differently coloured shapes firstly on to the ceiling and then radiating outwards and down on to all four walls. The lantern would then swing slightly, and could be gently rotated if one wished, so that the projected pattern moved around the hall. The effect of this could be mesmerising, and all that was missing were the unseen chimes and the pixie dust.

Chapter 8

My work at The Boynes was less stressful than it had been at Black Lake Cottage. Here there were no black moods, no prolonged silences, and I could speak more freely. I might have been corrected sometimes but always it was done politely. The Winters' marriage appeared to be a happy one and the domestic atmosphere was always cheery, though suitably restrained while students were present. And there were no hectic periods of entertaining, of course, but that meant that I missed the excitement of seeing, and sometimes speaking with, well-known personalities.

Working occasionally at Black Lake Cottage during the second quarter of 1904 meant that I saw Fred rarely and briefly and not as often as I should have liked. Our communications, as with so many others, were conducted mainly by letter or postcard. Medstead had a post office, run by blacksmith Thomas King, but that was almost two miles distant. Just a few hundred yards in the opposite direction, over the other side of the railway line, sparsely populated Four Marks was beginning to become developed, and there, across the road from The Windmill public house, was a new post office and shop which had just been fitted out at Four Marks House. They must have known I was coming! This was run by Mary Parsons and was my lifeline for a few years. You had to collect your post from there in those days; they didn't deliver it to your home. And for money orders everyone still had to go to Medstead. For telegrams, the nearest telegraph office was very close at hand, at the railway station. There was also a post box on the station platform which I found very handy.

I got around mostly on foot or by bicycle. Medstead had one other shop, as I recall: a grocer and draper store run by William Bond, but I didn't need to go there often. Other shops lay farther away, at Alton, and most goods were ordered from, and delivered by roundsmen with horse-drawn vans, just as at Black Lake Cottage.

A highlight of my time at Medstead was when Fred visited me for the first time. It was in mid July 1904, and he brought my friend Annie. The Winters were quite happy for me to entertain my friends at the Boynes so long as we respected their privacy, and on this occasion they were away from home. It was a warm, dry day and we spent much of the time lazing in the front garden and walking in the surrounding countryside. On our return from the walk I served tea for the three of us in the garden. I dared to use Mrs Winter's best china, and her silver tea service, and laid everything on two small lace-edged tablecloths. I wanted to impress my visitors, especially Fred. Fred had brought his new camera and the photographs taken that day were subsequently developed and printed as picture postcards by him back home in London. He later used them for writing to me, and he also sent some to Annie and me for our own use. On one of Fred and me, taken by Annie, I wrote to my young cousin (Josephine) Vera Baker, then a girl of eight: "How do you like this? Can you guess who this is? Shall I tell you? My s_____." I had longed to tell someone that I had a sweetheart, and I certainly could not have shared such secrets with my mother without fear of inquisition, and worse, for I had seen the effect she had had on my sister, Gwen. Gwen had had to give up her young man or move out. She did not move out. A selfless person, she devoted forty of her eighty-five years to caring for our mother and never saw another chance to marry.

In mid-August 1904, I started suffering from acute facial pains. There was no doctor in Medstead, and so a visit to Alton was necessary. There, the doctor diagnosed the cause of my pains as neuralgia. It so happened that the Winters were not going away for their main holiday and, as the Davies family were not spending the month at Tilford, as they had done for each August of the previous three years, the Barries had less than their usual need of my presence at Black Lake Cottage. In fact, Mr Barrie spent a good deal of his time there working on *Peter Pan*. I was therefore encouraged by my considerate employers to take a break myself, and I chose to return to Poole for a few weeks to get some sea air, and spend time with my family.

I didn't have much of a holiday but at least it was a change. The pain from the neuralgia was often excrutiating and, consequently, I missed visits to the Snooks in Winterborne Whitechurch and the Bakers in Milborne St Andrew. But one day was brightened considerably when I received a second picture postcard from Fred in five days. It was another of his Medstead photographs, and on the back of it he had written: 'Shall never forget the day when this was taken. "It might have been raining"'. Dear Fred. He had remembered some of my parting words to him on the platform of Medstead station at the end of our long, hazy, entirely rainless day together. Suddenly, I realised that it was not just my face that ached so much. How sad, though, that our correspondence had to be kept secret from my mother, for I had to arrange for Fred to write to me care of a friend, Ellen Godwin, who lived nearby.

Mercifully, the neuralgia went away as quickly as it had struck, and after a few enjoyable trips in the sunshine to some local coastal haunts including Lilliput, Sandbanks and Canford Cliffs, I was soon on my way back east eagerly anticipating a chance to see Fred. Alas, it was not to be. The Barries had just returned to London, and no more hosting at the cottage was planned until the following spring. For now, there was nothing for it but to knuckle down to the routine of my work at The Boynes and hope that other opportunities would arise for us to meet.

Chapter 9

The autumn and winter saw no furthering of my relationship with Fred, although I did manage to make a day trip up to London to see him for a few hours. And the spring of 1905 was no better. The Barries went to Normandy for Easter and, in June, Mrs Barrie went on a motoring trip in France with a friend. In between those jaunts across the Channel, Fred managed just a couple of visits to Medstead when he could be spared from his duties. Picnic lunch in basket, I met Fred off the train and we set off on walks - up to sixteen miles one day, taking in surrounding villages such as Chawton and Selborne. By then, I had acquired my own bicycle, and on one later visit, in mid July, Fred brought his bicycle and we rode way out into the Hampshire countryside. We went south to Hambledon, where the sport of cricket is said to have been raised to an art, and where the local team once famously beat the England team with ease. It was Fred's idea to show me Hambledon because he had driven Mr Barrie and E. V. Lucas there, for the two writers were great friends and devotees of the game, and Lucas had agreed to edit a book about cricket and the Hambledon players over the years. Titled *The Hambledon Men* and published in 1907, it included a new edition of John Nyren's book of 1833, *The Young Cricketer's Tutor*. Fred wanted to revisit Hambledon and be free to roam the area as he pleased, for he had been obliged to be present at all the Allahakbarries' matches since 1903 and had grown interested in the sport. Besides, cricket and photography were the only topics of conversation in which his famous passenger would engage him, if only very occasionally now, for Barrie didn't show any real interest in motor cars just so long as they conveyed him safely from A to B, and that was only when he had to use them.

Sadly, our visit to Hambledon and Broadhalfpenny Down proved to be our last glorious whole day together. While my association with the Barries and the Winters did not to draw to a close for over another year, opportunities for Fred and me to meet were increasingly denied us. Through the summer I had been told that my father was unwell. Then, one day in late August, I received worrying news that he was seriously ill, and there was a request that I return home to Mayflower quickly. Goodbye euphoria, hello harsh reality. A few days later, on September 1st, my dear father died of cerebral endarteritis at the age of seventy.

My father's death caused great sorrow throughout our large family, and for me it cast a giant shadow over the wonderful times I had enjoyed latterly. My mother, who by now was fifty-four and deaf, had seen five of her grown up children – Edgar, Harold, Wilfrid, Gwen and me - leave home to pursue their careers. She was left with one daughter, Lottie, who was a young teacher at a school nearby, and two sons, Hugh, aged fourteen, and Don, twelve, who were due back at school shortly to begin another year's education. These younger siblings of mine had witnessed our father's ailing and had supported our mother through some increasingly difficult times during the summer, and I decided that, for a few months at least, my place should be with them and my mother whenever I could manage it.

It took all of my earnings to make the frequent train journeys between Medstead and Poole. It also took all my spare days and left no scope for seeing Fred. But, if I was honest with myself, our relationship had not continued to blossom quite as I wished. Life, and the odds, seemed to be against us. I suppose we were not sufficiently mad about each other to make things happen regardless of any consequences. It was never easy, bearing in mind that we were fellow employees of the Barries, from whom we managed to keep our meetings a secret. At least, I think we did. Certainly, the matter was never raised by either of them.

During the autumn and winter of 1905 Mrs Barrie's single use of the car increased to the extent that it was she, rather than her husband, who was Fred's employer. Among other purposes, she used it to make visits to her mother in St Giles. Mrs Ansell, no longer at Hastings, had become very ill and she died early in

1906 and, in what had become a rare sight, Mr Barrie travelled with his wife in the car on the day of the funeral. I daresay I wouldn't have known about this were it not for my still being in contact with Fred by post. The Barries were still putting on a show to the outside world that they were a happily married couple, despite the growing difficulties within their marriage, and I feel sure that Mr Barrie would have made loving efforts to give support to his wife at that time. But his attempts would have stopped short of full intimacy and, by this time, would have been rejected if, by some miracle, such had been tried.

During 1905 Mrs Barrie had taken a studio in Kensington where she could pursue one of her interests: enamel-work. Now, in 1906, she continued to follow her own pursuits and was growing ever more independent of her husband. Crucially, for me, the social gatherings amid the pines at Black Lake Cottage started to decline. This was another indication that James and Mary Barrie were drifting apart.

Also, in June, it became known that Arthur Davies had developed a deep-seated sarcoma in the left side of his face and had had an operation to remove his upper jawbone, cheekbone, palate, teeth and tear duct on one side of his face. His prospects were poor. Grave concern for him dominated life for the Davieses, naturally, and for Barrie who, predictably, was incredibly supportive towards all of them, not least Arthur himself, with both his time and presence, cancelling commitments and functions and postponing his work for six weeks. He helped financially as well, but that was of no consequence to him. Through all of this the usual pattern of holidays and social gatherings was broken, with Barrie spending much time with the Davieses, not only at the hospital and nursing home but also at their home in Berkhamsted, and at Rustington where Sylvia's mother, Emma du Maurier, had rented a large house for August. Barrie was at Black Lake Cottage for a few days at the beginning of July but he had cancelled his cricket week and it was now a thing of the past. August at the cottage was like none before. Mr Barrie did spend a few odd days there but Mrs Barrie went on an extended motoring holiday in France.

While requirements for Fred's services increased, those for mine became unpredictable and unsettling. My train journeys between Medstead and Farnham were being made at ever shorter notice and things reached an unsatisfactory point where, for half the year, I no longer knew where I would be from one week to the next. It was nobody's fault, least of all that of the Winters. It was the way things were, and I couldn't see the situation improving. Besides, for over three years I had lived in rural locations and had enjoyed virtually no social life. All in all, by the end of August, I decided it was probably time to consider moving on.

The next few months would see me acquire a position in Wrexham, in North Wales, where there would be stability in the house of a clothier and shopkeeper, William Thomas, and his wife Elizabeth. I got the job through his daughter, Gwendolen Thomas, who was a Cambridge graduate in Literature, and who tutored in London and was an acquaintenance of Mr Barrie in Kensington. There, in Wrexham, I would soon discover the greatest love of my life. Later, I would suffer hardship and sorrow such as I had never known, and would never know again. And from there, in 1917, I would return again to Poole, needing help from my family. And twice more in my life as a housekeeper I would venture away from Dorset for periods of years, only to return again.

But all of that lay in the future. This was now, and I felt the need to be with my family on the first anniversary of my father's death. Upon my arrival at Mayflower I found all my immediate family there and it was an emotional time, and one of much reminiscing. Sharing my current problems with my siblings in the evening helped me to see everything clearly, and I made my decision to make a clean break of things and start afresh. I needed to write some letters, and I would do that the next morning.

The morning came sooner than I expected. After just a couple of hours' sleep I awoke in the middle of the night and couldn't get back to sleep again. I found myself thinking about my father, about cutting myself off from Fred, and about inconveniencing the Barries and the Winters. I even started thinking about the

Davies boys and what the future might hold for them should their father die. After allowing all these thoughts due time and respect I tried to blank them out and get some sleep, but it was hopeless. Eventually, I realised that I was probably going to continue in this wretched state all night, and so I decided there was only one thing to do, and I went downstairs and made a cup of tea. Wide awake now, and alone in the kitchen of the silent house, I wrote my letter to Fred, explaining everything and telling him of my decision. Then, still far from sleepy but knowing I was tired, I decided to dress and go out for some fresh air, thinking that a little walk might do the trick.

Ignoring the drizzle, I strolled on damp, lamplit pavements down Longfleet Road and into the top of the High Street. I bade final farewell to Fred at the post box outside the post office. I then crossed the street and veered left down Park Lane, past the School of Art and Technology, past the iron and brass Foundry, and straight on down to the harbour by the shortest route. Once at New Quay, I turned right, along East Quay Road, until, close by the Poole Pottery works, I found a favourite seat facing the water. Unwittingly, my walk had been a brush with the future, for my brother, Hugh, would become Head of Poole School of Art and Technology; my eldest stepson, George Steer Jones, would spend most of his working life employed at Poole Foundry; and, following studying art at the School of Art, my daughter, Marian, would be a paintress at Poole Pottery. Had I been blessed with clairvoyance my spirits might have been lifted higher and higher as I approached the harbour. I might have seen, too, that the greatest love and happiness in my life, for a precious few years anyway, stood just a northward train journey away. As it was, I was downhearted, for I was overwhelmed by the emotion of great loss and of deliberately ending a chapter in my life.

It was still dark. It wouldn't be dawn for a while yet. The drizzle had turned to light rain but it didn't bother me. I sat down and gazed vacantly in the direction of Brownsea Island, and the sky and I cried gently together.

Epilogue

Granny read a lot and liked happy endings, and so I should like you to finish this story with a smile on your face.

In September 1901 James Barrie paid a visit to Rupert Darnley Anderson, the Liverpool-born, retired fruit broker and owner of Waverley Abbey House and its estate. The purpose of the visit is not known but Barrie was moved to make a lengthy and priceless entry in the Andersons' visitors book which I now reproduce with the kind permission of Andrew Birkin. I have corrected the odd inconsistent use of punctuation and underlining by Barrie; scans of Barrie's three handwritten pages may be accessed on Andrew's website. In the wake of the recent film starring Johnny Depp, Kate Winslet, Julie Christie and Dustin Hoffman, I cannot resist prefixing Barrie's title with one of my own.

Never Finding Land Enough for Delphiniums

Or

Rupert and Mary - Or, What it is Coming To

(1) Dear Mr Anderson,
   I find Black Lake Cottage delightful. All it needs to be a perfect cottage is a paling which would be made of the trees in the wood. May I cut some down? Yours, M.B.

(2) Dear Mrs Barrie,
   Yes, by all means. You can take a hundred trees. Yours, R.A.

(3) Dear Mr Anderson,
 Thank you so much. I have cut down the thousand trees you offered me so kindly. How charming the wood is. May I lift my fence and put it round a few acres of wood? M.B.

(4) Dear Mrs Barrie,
 Certainly. R.A.

(5) Dear Mr Anderson,
 I have been much struck by the beauty of the Black Lake and feel sure I could do something with it. May I put my fence round it? Thanking you in advance. Yours M.B.

(6) Dear Mrs Barrie,
 That will be all right. Is there anything else you would care to have? R.A.

(7) Dear Mr Anderson,
 As you are so kind, might I have the abbey ruins? They are just what (I) want for my larkspurs. M.B.

(8) Dear Mrs Barrie,
 By all means put your fence round the abbey ruins. R.A.

(9) Dear Mr Anderson,
 Is not Waverley too big for you? I should so like to add it in my little property. M.B.

(10) Dear Mrs Barrie,
 Waverley is yours. R.A.

(11) Dear Mr Anderson,
 What a handsome little boy you have got. May I put my fence round him? M.B.

(12) Dear Mrs Barrie,
I have decided it best to put the matter into the hands of Mrs Anderson. (R.A.)

(13) Madam,
   I am coming round at once to put a fence round <u>you</u>. Amy D. K. Anderson.

End of Correspondence

Yours sincerely,
J. M. Barrie.

Appendix

Fact or fiction?

Without wishing to spoil what, I hope, will have been an enjoyable read, it is only fair that I come clean over the fictional elements of Mabel's story as told by me. It would be irresponsible of me to mislead or misinform anyone, not least Barriephiles and researchers into J. M. Barrie's life and times or, indeed, into the lives of the other persons mentioned in this book. While I was lucky to know my grandmother, albeit forty years ago, I knew little about Barrie until six months ago. I am not a historian and this is my first stab at writing a book.

I did not intend to write this book. I was going to write an article and submit it to my local newspaper in the hope that they might print it in conjunction with the inevitable publicity for the Christmas pantomime at my home town's theatre. December 2004 was going to be the centenary of the first performance of *Peter Pan*, and I had discovered that the local pantomime was to be *Peter Pan*. There would never be a better time to tell my granny's story. And who would tell it but me? A telephone call to the newspaper confirmed that they would be interested in my article and that they might be able to give it half a page, including any photographs. I concluded that the article was going to take a day or two to research, and a day to write. I set myself a tight deadline. How naïve of me.

I started with few facts. My first research session led, unexpectedly, to a desire to look deeper into the subject. Self-imposed rescheduled deadlines came and went, and it soon became clear that a brief article simply would not satisfy me. Nor could it do justice to my granny or to Barrie. A long article, then? One closer to my admitted verbose style? No. Who would have room for one? Who would take one from an unknown and inexperienced writer? The Sunday glossy supplements? Fat chance. I considered looking for an agent or a publisher but that way lay delay and very probable rejection, again and again. Wasn't that what happened to everyone? In any case, this was going to be a one-off effort, for I was retired and had lots of things I wanted to do. I was not seeking to establish myself as a writer.

December was almost upon me; it was all too late; I should have embarked on this diversion months earlier. One thing was certain: I was not going to hand all my hard-won knowledge to someone else to play with, and I could see that there could be a lot of fun delving further, making more contacts, visiting people and places, discussing, pondering and speculating, and then finally writing something. But what, exactly? It was going to have to be a book, that much was clear. Maybe a small one, of narrow appeal, but no matter. I had a story to tell, and I was the one who was going to tell it. It was my bone! Furthermore, foolhardy perhaps, I decided I was going to publish and sell the book myself, for I was enjoying 'an awfully big adventure'.

The engineer and manager in me influenced the process, and this approach applied no less to writing the story. I mapped out the events chronologically and spatially, if not geographically, and proceeded to link them. There were basically two timelines, Mabel's and Barrie's, which met, ran closely parallel between April 1903 and some unknown point in time around or not long after the summer of 1906, and then diverged. At intervals there were specific meeting points on the parallel section. Then there were other linking timelines. The picture in my mind was akin to the London Underground map devised by Harry Beck, though with added dimensions. The coincidence of the District and Central Lines between the Gloucester Road and Tower Hill stations represented Mabel's time with the Barries. Thus Gloucester Road station represented her first meeting with Barrie, South Kensington the hat-box episode, Victoria the 1903 cricket week, and so on. But a two-dimensional model was inadequate, so I wrapped it around the surface of a hollow, transparent sphere to enable third dimension elements to be added and sometimes cross-connected: elements like interrelationships and coincidences. Another dimension was needed for the thoughts and suggestions which derived from those and, for this, my brain could come up with only simple labelled boxes and tags. Is this how writers work? Or is such a complex and methodical approach necessary only when attempting to combine biography with fiction, when the writer is anxious to avoid discrepancies and anomalies in the quest to tell a credible story.

Oh, the worry! As I approach the printing stage, the point of no return – as I write these very words, in fact – I start to be concerned that justice has been done to the subject, or subjects, and that, despite all the revisions and amendments, the additions and deletions, and the rewrites, nothing has been written that can be discredited. What errors and omissions will be spotted by the knowledgible reader who, like Bill Bryson finding a flaw with the London Underground map, will then announce it to the world with a whoop of delight? Within his book *Notes From a Small Island*, Bryson wrote: 'an out-of-town visitor using Mr Beck's map to get from, say, Bank Station to Mansion House, would quite understandably board a Central Line train to Liverpool Street, transfer to the Circle Line and continue for another five stops to Mansion House, at which point they would emerge 200 yards down the street from the location they'd started at.' If that is true then, while it is amusing to some, especially to me, doubtless it is annoying to those visitors who have been misled. In an attempt to avoid similar fault-finding by any of my readers I hurled my transparent globe into space, set it rotating, and observed its content from an orbiting satellite. I wonder what discrepancies I failed to see.

These, then, are the main aspects of my story for which insufficient evidence could be found to enable me to endorse them as fact:

1 Fred, Mabel's sweetheart who lived in London and evidently was 'new' to her life, has been assumed to be Frederick, the Barries' chauffeur between 1903 and 1908. It is the most likely

possibility, and it provided a useful thread for the story. The evidence is in a number of 1904/1905 photo-postcards which Mabel kept or recovered from from others to whom she had written some. These are in my family's possesion; I used one for the cover of this book. As I could be mistaken, I kept the relationship low-key, with no blame attaching to Fred for anything. No-one in my family has any knowledge of who Fred really was. With Mabel largely confined to her rural workplaces, we could not think of any more likely answer to the question: How did she manage, in 1903 or 1904, to meet someone named Fred who lived in London? Prior to moving to Black Lake Cottage, she had lived in North Wales since June 1900, and then in deepest Dorset. I would dearly love to be contacted by anyone with information about Fred or Frederick, be they two distinct gentlemen or one and the same.

2 The precise time of Mabel starting and finishing work with the Barries. By reference to the 1953 magazine article *Barrie and Hanny*, and also to the biographies of Barrie, though sadly not the actual job advert which I was unable to find, Mabel had to have started sometime between early April 1903 (her grandfather died on 1 April) and the end of June 1903 (the Black Lake Cottage cricket week), and certainly by August 1903 (her recollection of the bear hunt game in the woods with Barrie and the Davies boys establishes this). Again, from information in the 1953 article and the biographies, Mabel had to have been at Black Lake Cottage when Robert Falcon Scott visited (which seems to have been in the spring or summer of 1906), but she must have moved to Wrexham not long after that - I would say by 1907 at the latest, given that she married a widowed man with 4 children there in April 1910. Her husband had been a postman there since starting work, and his first wife died in 1907. That Mabel also lived and worked at Barrie's sister Maggie's home at Medstead is evidenced by items of personal correspondence, including the envelopes, in the familiy's possession, the crucial item being a letter addressed to her at The Boynes in January 1904 in which the writer expresses a hope that Mabel had settled

into her new home there.

3   How Barrie came to purchase his first Lanchester. My research led me to a likely scenario, what with both the English Locomobile Company and Archibald Millarship being based in Kensington (from whom Barrie almost certainly would have bought his steam car in 1901), and Millarship moving, still in London, to the Lanchester company as their chief demonstrator in about 1902.

4   James Hook! Fact or fiction? Here's what happened during my research: I wanted to try and find out who were the 'Frensham Artists' who, according to some biographies, played cricket matches against the Allahabarries in 1903, 1904 and 1905, defeating them in 1903 and 1904. This quest might have enabled me to find and include some new information concerning Barrie and those matches. I first tried consulting the present Frensham Cricket Club, and also a local historian at Frensham, but this produced nothing of real use.

   I then searched through the 1901 census for the entire parish of Frensham whereupon I was relieved to find no less than six artists living in then small village of Churt. That gave me six possible names for some of the cricketers. Only five more and I would have a team! But it was not that simple. One of the six was a woman, and so, without being sexist, I thought it was reasonable to discount her. One was aged eighty-one. One was aged fifty-three and, by the time he was fifty-five, would possibly have considered himself to be too old to play. The other three were between one and seven years older than Barrie. Of those three, two had the surname of Hook and were born, of all places, in Kensington. These Hook men lived with their respective families at different addresses in Churt. I soon established, from earlier censuses and the General Register Office's indexes of registered births, that they were brothers: Allan James Hook and Bryan Hook. Not only that, but the elderly artist in the parish was their famous father, James Clarke Hook, RA, who was still painting in 1905, two years before his death. Perhaps he was also still playing cricket, but that seems too much to believe. Research at the Farnham Museum revealed that the *Farnham Herald* carried a report of the 1905 match but not of the earlier ones.

From the biographies, it is evident that Barrie came up with the name of James Hook for his pirate captain in *Peter Pan* some time in 1904. I therefore put two and two together and made, I think, four. If I am mistaken, then all I can say is I stumbled upon a most amazing coincidence. I then contacted the present owner of Silverdale, the large house where James Clarke Hook lived (Hook built it, actually), but there seemed to be no relevant remnants of the artist and his artist sons.

It would be remiss of me to finish this explanation without adding that I found there were two other theories about Barrie's choice of the name for the fictional captain, although I have to say that they deal only with the surname. When he was a boy in Kirriemuir, the young James Barrie had been scared by the sight of a man with a metal hook in place of his hand, and that man was a cart-driver known as 'Hooky' Crewe - Barrie wrote about him in *Auld Licht Idylls*. In *The Little White Bird* the author created a schoolmaster character named Pilkington and he had a hook.

I can offer two more ideas: In the garden at Black Lake Cottage a butcher nicknamed 'Hookie' supplied goldfish for the pond, and a tree in the garden was named 'Hookie's Tree', after Mrs Barrie's first tortoise which was tethered to it. (Another tree was later named 'Everard's Tree' after the second tortoise, the one which replaced Hookie after Luath had tipped it onto its back and left it to die of hunger or dehydration).

There is yet another possibility: When quizzed about Hook, Barrie once said: "Hook was not his true name. To reveal who he really was would even at this date set the country ablaze." It has been hypothesised that his Captain Hook was modelled after the famous English naval officer, Captain Christopher Newport. Both were dark-haired, of dubious pasts and were missing their right hands which were replaced by a metal hook. It is tempting to think that Newport was the inspiration. Furthermore, Newport commanded the ships that landed the settlers at Jamestown in Virginia, USA. Yes, Jamestown. Could this name have led to the choice of James for Hook's first name? Or could Barrie have simply given him his own name?

Perhaps, as Andrew Birkin and others have said, Barrie amalgamated several Hooks into one new character. While Barrie admitted that he based the character on a famous person whose identity he never revealed, was his choice of name for the character mere coincidence or was it inspired typically by someone in his life, or, again typically, by an amalgamation of several of them?

5 Elaboration of the bear hunt game: This game was described briefly in the *Barrie and Hanny* article, and I have taken that as a reliable source and merely fleshed out the account in order to create an amusing episode which, given the published accounts of other such games in the lake and pinewoods in August 1901, 1902 and 1903, may not be too far from the actual game played.

6 Fred and Mabel's trip to Hambledon. I know, from the 1904/1905 postcards, that the couple walked and cycled together from The Boynes. They must have gone somewhere other than merely Chawton and Selborne, both quite near to Medstead. Hambledon was only twelve miles distant and, in my view, would have been an obvious choice for a cycling trip.

7 Barrie and Lucas's trip to Hambledon. This could well have happened at any time, but quite possibly during the period in June 1905 when Barrie had his car and when the Lucases stayed at Black Lake Cottage for, it seems, about a fortnight. Lucas brought out his book on the Hambledon cricketers in 1907, and Barrie had some connection with cricket at Hambledon, although I could not get at anything concrete. He mentioned Broadhalfpenny Down in *The Little White Bird*, of course, and, very recently, in 1999, Barrie and Lucas together were made posthumous members of the revived Hambledon Club (which nust mean something, but the Club would not, or could not, tell

me exactly why Barrie was included. Very strange, but then while there is a committee, etc, this club seems to be little more than an exclusive dining club based in Hambledon).

Here is a little more information relevant to my story. The 1901 Census for the parish of Frensham revealed the following persons as artists:

James C Hook, 81, Artist Painter, born Clerkenwell (James Clarke Hook, R.A.)
Allan J Hook, 48, Retired Artist & Painter, born Kensington (Allan James Hook)
Bryan Hook, 45, Artist & Painter, born Kensington
Ernold Mason, 42, Book Illustrator, born Sydenham (Ernold A Mason)
Ellen E Mason, 44, Miniature Painter, born Hatcham (wife of Ernold Mason)
William B Gardner, 53, Artist Sculptor, born London

Finally, my information concerning Mary Ansell which is relevant to my story but which may be of more interest to researchers into Barrie's life:

My discovery that Mary Ansell was only 10 months younger than Barrie, instead of almost seven years younger, seems to have come as a revelation in the present world of J. M. Barrie. I checked and double-checked my findings before announcing this information to the J. M. Barrie Society, Nottingham University (whose collection of D. H. Lawrence letters had reference to Mary Cannan's birth year as 1867) and others. Is this news significant, especially so long after the event? I suggest that it is of interest to anyone engaged in examining the life and works of Barrie, his relationship with Mary Ansell and the failure of their fifteen-year marriage, for it casts some new light thereon. It seems to me that Barrie took the blame for the failure of the marriage, and that, until her adultery, his wife was depicted as blameless. Now that we know that Mary seems to have lied to

Barrie, and certainly lied to some authorities - for she was still deceiving them at the time of the 1901 census, and again in 1910 on the occasion of her second marriage - it is possible to imagine that there may have been other deceptions, and thus a darker side to her.

The King's Head, where Mary was born on March 1st 1861, was at 71 Moscow Road, Paddington. From The King's Head, the family moved to 137 Westbourne Park Road, Paddington. After Mary's father, George Ansell, died Mary moved with her mother to 113 Mount Pleasant Road, Hastings. Mary's presence with her parents was recorded in the 1861 Census, when she was one month old, and the 1871 Census, when she was ten years old. In the 1881 Census, when she was living with her mother, her age was stated as twenty years. Her birth certificate shows her mother's maiden name was Mary Kitchen. Her marriage certificate to Barrie also shows that her mother's maiden name was Mary Kitchen. There is no doubting that this was the same Mary Ansell who married J. M. Barrie.

But, as I have said, in adulthood Mary lied about her age. She married Barrie on July 9th 1894 at which time she was thirty-three. On her marriage certificate her age is stated as twenty-seven whereas Barrie's age is correctly stated as thirty-four. On the 1901 Census return (on the night of 31st March 1901), Mary's age is stated as thirty-four, not forty, whereas Barrie's age is correctly stated as forty.

Mary also lied, it seems, about her place of birth. Her birth certificate states that she was born in Paddington, London. The 1901 Census return states that she was born in Northwood, Middlesex, at that time a village in a rural area twelve miles north-west of her actual place of birth which was correctly recorded in the earlier censuses.

About six months following her divorce from Barrie, Mary married Gilbert Cannan, on April 28th 1910. The marriage certificate states that her age was forty-one years. She was actually forty-nine at the time, and so she had trimmed a further two years off her age. The twenty-five year-old Cannan's prospects for any children to result from the marriage clearly were nowhere near as good as he may have expected. There were no children, and in 1918 this marriage also ended in divorce, this time as a result of adultery committed by Gilbert Cannan..

As for Barrie's play *Rosalind*, not only does this seem to reveal that, by 1912 at the latest, the playwright knew Mary had deceived him over her age, but it was curiously prophetic. At one point we are told that the young woman is at Monte Carlo, "a place where people gamble," and elsewhere we learn that she was supposed to be spending a month in Biarritz. How strange that in February 1921 D. H. Lawrence should write to Mary Cannan expressing disapproval of her gambling and advising her that she should not let it become a habit, and that some time after 1925 Mary left England permanently to live the rest of her life in Biarritz, where she died in July 1950 at the age of eighty-nine.

At what stage did Barrie discover he had been lied to by Mary about her age? If this was during their marriage, was he happy to perpetuate that lie? And if he was, then why? He had married a very pretty woman; everyone knew that. Did he believe he had married a woman much younger than himself to boot? It seems everyone else did. Or did Barrie know the truth from the outset? All future biographies of J. M. Barrie, and other studies concerning Barrie's life and his works, should have regard to this facet of his fascinating life.

Sources

UNPUBLISHED SOURCES
Some picture postcards sent to and from Mabel Lewellyn in 1904 and 1905.
Family history research of The Llewellyn and Snook families carried out by David Greenham and Shirley Firth, with additional research in 2004 by Robert Greenham.

PUBLISHED SOURCES
A selection of Barrie's works:
Alice Sit-by-the-Fire; *Auld Licht Idylls*, *Dear Brutus*; *The Little White Bird*; *Peter & Wendy*; *Peter Pan*; *Rosalind*; *Sentimental Tommy*; *What Every Woman Knows*; (Hodder & Stoughton); *The Greenwood Hat* (Peter Davies).

Selective bibliography:
ANSELL, Mary: *The Happy Garden* (Cassell, 1912)
ASQUITH, Cynthia: *Portrait of Barrie* (James Barrie, 1954)
BEETON, Isabella: *Mrs Beeton's Book of Household Management* (Ward, Lock & Co Ltd., 1906)
BIRKIN, Andrew: *J. M. Barrie and the Lost Boys* (Constable and Company, 1979)
CROW, Duncan: *The Edwardian Woman* (George Allen & Unwin, 1978)
DARLINGTON, W. A.: *J. M. Barrie* (Blackie, 1938)
DUNBAR, Janet: *J. M. Barrie: The Man Behind the Image* (Collins, 1970)
KIPLING, Rudyard: *Steam Tactics* (1902), collected in *Traffics and Discoveries* (MacMillan, 1904)
LONG, Helen C: *The Edwardian House – The Middle-class Home in Britain, 1880-1914* (Manchester University Press, 1993)
MACKAIL, Denis: *The Story of J. M. B.* (Peter Davies, 1941)

MILLS, Betty: *Four Marks: its Life and Origins* (Repton Publishing, 1995)

MINGAY, G. E.: *Rural Life in Victorian England* (Sutton Publishing, 1976)

LORD MONTAGUE OF BEAULIEU & BIRD, Anthony: *Steam Cars 1779-1970* (Cassell, 1971)

MOORE, Harry T.: *The Collected Letters of D. H. Lawrence* (Heinemann, 1962)

PERKINS, Joan: *Victorian Women* (John Murray, 1993)

QUENNELL, Marjorie and C. H. B, revised by Peter Quennell: *A History of Everyday Things in England, 1851-1914*, (B. T. Batsford Ltd, 1958)

SHAW, Bernard: *The Man with Hell in his Soul* (Sunday Graphic and Sunday News, June 20, 1937)

STEINBECK, Susie: *Women in England 1760-1914 – A Social History* (Weidenfeld & Nicolson, 2004)

THOMAS, Gwendolen: *'Barrie and Hanny'* (John o' London's Weekly, June 5, 1953)

IT MIGHT HAVE BEEN RAINING

ERRATA

MAJOR (factual)
Page 10, line 10: for 'Joe Gramm' read 'Ron Paolillo'
Page 61, line 19: for 'Kirriemuir' read 'Bothwell'
Page 46, line 33: for 'Silverdale' read 'Silverbeck'
Page 84, line 22: for 'George' read 'Ernest'
Page 94, line 10: for 'Silverdale' read 'Silverbeck'

MINOR (mainly typographical)
Page 06, line 03: for 'adbominal' read 'abdominal'
Page 13, line 17: for 'monastry' read 'monastery'
Page 15, line 05: for 'farmouse' read 'farmhouse'
Page 27, line 02: for 'mantlepiece' read 'mantelpiece'
Page 28, line 31: for 'conspicuouly' read 'conspicuously'
Page 28, line 37: for 'comforable' read 'comfortable'
Page 34, line 35: for 'Flint House' read 'cottage'
Page 50, line 34: delete the first 'the'
Page 52, line 18: for 'relevation' read 'revelation'
Page 55, line 26: for 'publically' read 'publicly'
Page 57, line 05: for 'glamourous' read 'glamorous'
Page 62, line 11: for 'lead' read 'led'
Page 66, line 37: for 'frend' read 'friend'
Page 83, line 16: for 'acquaintenance' read 'acquaintance'
Page 91, line 15: for 'knowledgible' read 'knowledgeable'
Page 92, line 04: for 'possesion' read 'possession'
Page 92, line 35: for 'familiy's' read 'family's'
Page 95, line 35: for 'nust' read 'must'

Index

In compiling the index for this book I have been mindful, and hopeful, that there will be more than one class of reader, not least the many members of the Llewellyn clan. The book is biographical mainly in respect of Mabel Llewellyn, but necessarily incorporates concise biographies of James Barrie and Mary Ansell which include a few snippets of what I believe is new information and fresh thought. It is also a snapshot of life one hundred years ago, and the whole blend has been seasoned with a little imagination to create a pseudo-autobiographical story. Thus, while the index to the resulting potpourri may appear to include trivial entries, please bear in mind that it attempts to be all things to all readers.

Abbey, Edwin, 47
Admirable Crichton, The (Barrie), 20, 43
Alfred (the Barries' 1st chauffeur), 43
Alice Sit-by-the-Fire (Barrie), 45, 59
Allahakbarries, 40, 43, 46, 47, 80, 92
Alphonse (the Barries' 3rd chauffeur), 43
Alresford, 21, 69, 75
Alton, 21, 69, 70, 77
Amundsen, Roald, 35
Anderson, Amy D. K., 87
Anderson, Elizabeth Garrett, 55
Anderson, Rupert Darnley, 24, 32, 85
Annals, William, 68
Annie, 78
Anon. A Play (Barrie), 66
Ansell, George Jnr, 36
Ansell, George Snr, 36, 96
Ansell, Mary (later Barrie, then Cannan), 21, 24, 27, 31, 34, 36, 41, 44, 49, 57, 60, 64, 74, 81, 82, 85, 94, 96
Ansell, Mary (wife of George Snr.) *See* Kitchen Mary
Ansell, Thomas, 36
Ansell, William, 36
Arch, Joseph, 17, 38
Archer, Thomas, 43
Artists, 46
Atkins, Mary, 42
Auld Licht Idylls (Barrie), 94
Austen, Jane, 69
Australia, 17

Baker, (Josephine) Vera, 78
Bakers, the, 79
Baldwin, Stanley, 35, 36
Ball, Rosamund ('Graham R. Tomson'), 46
Ballard Down, 11
Bangor (Wales), 17
Barrie, David Jnr, 61
Barrie, David Snr, 6, 61
Barrie, James Matthew, 5, 6, 7, 11, 16, 20 21, 23, 27, 31, 32, 34, 36, 40, 46, 49, 53, 55, 60, 61, 66, 67, 72, 74, 78, 80, 82, 83, 85, 89, 90, 92, 95, 96
Barrie, Margaret ('Maggie') (later Winter), 6, 61, 71, 72, 74, 76, 78, 92
Barrie, Mary – *See* Ansell, Mary
Barries, the, 18, 21, 25, 42, 49, 53, 57, 67, 65, 67, 69, 75, 76, 78, 80, 81, 83, 88, 90, 96
Barrie and Hanny (Thomas), 92, 95
Barrie Lamp, the, 75
Barrie's Bank, 34
Barrymore, Ethel, 45, 46
Bayswater, 36
Bear hunt game, 57, 92, 95
Beeton, Mrs, 37
Benslow House, 59
Bentall, Alfred, 41
Bentall, Charles, 42
Bentalls, 42
Berkhamsted, 82
Biarritz, 98
Birrell, Augustine, 35, 46
Bisgood, Jeanne, 6
Black, Clementina, 55
Black Lake, 13, 34, 57, 69, 86
Black Lake Cottage, 6, 13, 20, 21, 22, 25, 31, 37, 39, 40, 43, 49, 53, 57, 60, 63, 65, 67, 69, 75, 77, 78, 82, 85, 92, 95

102

Black Lake Cricket Week, 40, 43, 45, 82, 92, 97
Blandford Forum, 15
Bodichon, Barbara, 55
Bond, William, 77
Booth, William, 17
Boucicault, Nina, 53
Bournemouth, 16
Box Hill, 34
Boynes, The, 15, 68, 69, 70, 74, 77, 92, 95
Bracknell, Lady, 52
Broadhalfpenny Down, 80, 95
Broadway (New York), 34, 45
Brownsea Island, 84
Bruce, Kathleen, 35
Burns, Robert, 56
Buxton, Rupert, 64

Cambridge, 55
Cambridge University, 55, 72, 73
Campbell, Mrs Patrick, 52
Cane, Jessie, 23, 28
Cane, John, 23
Cane, William (the Barries' gardener), 23, 31, 33, 41, 50
Canford Cliffs, 79
Cannan, Gilbert, 50, 97
Cannan, Mary – *See* Ansell, Mary
Castleman's Corkscrew, 15
Chawton, 69, 80, 95
Chess for Match Players (Winter), 73
Churt, 46, 93
City of London Chess Club, 73
Clapton Training College, 16
Clare College, Cambridge, 72, 73
College for Women, 55
Collett, Clara, 55
Crewe, 'Hooky', 94
Cricket, 40, 80, 92

Crompton, Mary (later Davies), 55
Cuthullin, 56

Daily Worker, 73
Davies, Arthur Llewelyn, 9, 53, 63, 82
Davies, George Llewelyn, 52, 53, 56, 61, 63
Davies, John Llewelyn ('Jack'), 53, 56, 61, 64
Davies, Revd John Llewelyn, 54, 63
Davies, Margaret Caroline, 55
Davies, Maurice Llewelyn, 63
Davies, Michael Llewelyn, 62, 63
Davies, Nicholas Llewelyn ('Nico'), 62, 64, 66
Davies, Peter Llewelyn, 56, 61, 64
Davies, Sarah Emily, 55
Davies, Sylvia - *See* Du Maurier, Sylvia
Davies, William Stephen, 55
Davies boys, 9, 57, 63, 84, 92
Davies family, 9, 53, 59, 66, 67, 78, 82
Dawson, Eleanor, 63
Dear Brutus (Barrie), 60, 62
Denmark Hill, 47
Dorchester, 17, 38
Du Maurier, Daphne, 54
Du Maurier, Emma, 82
Du Maurier, George Louis Palmella Busson, 54
Du Maurier, Gerald, 20 45, 53, 54
Du Maurier, Sylvia Jocelyn Busson (later Davies), 9, 53, 62, 66
Duke, Elsie, 71
Duke of York's Theatre, 7, 20, 75
Dumfries Academy, 6
Durrant, Ada, 77
Durrant, Charles ('Charlie'), 70

103

East Dulwich, 16
East Malling, 6
Edinburgh, 67
Edinburgh Infirmary, 67
Edinburgh University, 6
Embleton, Alfred ('Alfie'), 25
English Locomobile Company, 43, 92
Esher, 47
Everard, 94

Fanny, 60
Farm Workers Union, 17
Farnham, 6, 13, 21, 41, 45, 57, 59, 69, 70, 83
Farnham Herald, 94
Farnham Park, 47
Farnham railway station, 21, 69
Farnham Rural District Council, 60
Fingal (Ossian), 56
Fitt, Alice, 72
Flanders, 63
Flint Cottage, 34
Ford, Henry J, 48
Four Feathers, The (Mason), 45
Four Marks, 77
Four Marks House, 77
Fowey, 74
Frederick ('Fred')
  (the Barries' 2nd chauffeur), 7, 43, 57, 65, 69, 77, 78, 79, 80, 81, 83, 88, 91, 95
Frensham, 40, 46, 50, 93, 96
Frensham Artists, 46, 65, 92, 96
Frith, Walter, 45
Frohman, Charles, 34, 66
Fry, C(harles) B(urgess), 40

Gardner, William B., 96
Gilmour, Thomas, 46

Girton College, Cambridge, 55
Godwin, Ellen, 79
Goldsmith, Edward, 42
Golf-croquet, 31, 35, 40
Gosling, (Esther) Annie, 42
Gosling, (Mary) Jane, 42
Graham, Captain Harry, 45, 46
Great White Father, The (Barrie), 66
Green Hill, Farnham, 22
Greenhill Farm, 22
Greenham, Robert, 12
Greenwood, Frederick, 33
Greenwood Hat, The (Barrie), 33
Greenwood Hat-box, 32
Grey, Alice, 59
Grey, Colonel Robert, 59

Hackney, 16
Hambledon, 80, 95
Hambledon Club, 95
Hambledon Men, The (Lucas), 80
Hann, Arthur George, 6, 53
Hann, Mabel Bessie
  See Llewellyn, Mabel Bessie
Hann, Walter, 53
Hardy, Thomas, 17, 38, 46
Harper, Elizabeth, 63
Hastings, 36, 97
Hat-box, 32
Henley, Hannah Johnson (née Boyle), 66
Henley, Margaret Emma, 66
Henley, W(illiam) E(rnest), 66
Herrington, Flora, 71
Hewlett, Hilda, 45, 62
Hewlett, Maurice, 45, 62
Higher Whatcombe, 14, 20, 38
Hindhead, 60
Hitchin, 59
Hodgson, Mary, 63

Holland, Frederick, 70
Holland, William, 70
Hook, Allan James, 46, 93, 96
Hook, Bryan, 46, 93, 96
Hook, Captain James, 8, 47, 92, 94
Hook, James Clarke, 46, 93, 96
Hookie, 94
'Hooky' Crewe, 94
Hope, Anthony, 46
Hope, Elizabeth, 46
Horne, Edgar, 40
Hunt, ? (the Barries' gardener), 50
Hunt, George (the Lewises' gardener), 24, 51
Hunt, Kate (daughter of George), 24, 51
Hunt, Kate (wife of the Barries' gardener), 50
Hurricane Island (Marriott Watson), 46

Importance of Being Earnest, The (Wilde), 52
Isle of Purbeck, 11
Isle of Wight, 11

Jacomb-Hood, George Percy, 47
Jamestown, 95
John O' London's Weekly, 7
Jones, Archibald Ellis ('Archie'), 5, 92
Jones, George Steer, 84
Jones, James Llewelyn ('Jim'), 5, 41
Jones, Mabel Bessie ('May')
  See Llewellyn, Mabel Bessie
Jones, Marian Llewelyn ('Topsy'), 5, 41, 84
Jude the Obscure (Hardy), 38

Kennel (Porthos's & Luath's), 23
Kensington, 42, 43, 46, 53, 82, 83, 92, 93
Kensington Gardens, 53
King, Thomas, 77
King's Head, The, 36, 96
Kinge, Henry James, 59
Kinge, Isabel ('Doll')
  See Lamport, Isabel Kinge
Kinge, Myrtle Joyce, 60
Kings of Chess (Winter), 73
Kingston upon Thames, 42
Kipling, Rudyard, 43
Kirkby Lonsdale, 63
Kirriemuir, 6, 16, 61, 94
Kitchen, Mary (later Ansell), 36, 81, 96
Kitty Hawk, 68

La Thangue, Henry Herbert, 47
Lambeth, 53
Lamport, Alice Joyce (later Kinge), 25, 31, 32, 39, 44, 43, 49, 55, 59, 71
Lamport, Fanny (later Embleton), 25, 60
Lamport, Isabel Kinge ('Doll'), 59
Lanchester (car), 43, 55, 81, 92
Lang, Andrew, 46
Lark Ascending, The (Meredith), 11
Lawrence, D(avid) H(erbert), 64, 96, 98
Leinster Corner, 42, 68, 75
Lewis, Anna, 23
Lewis, Henry, 23, 51
Lewis, Jane, 23
Lilliput, 79
Little Mary (Barrie), 53
Little Newcastle, 21
Little White Bird, The (Barrie), 16, 19, 59, 94, 95

Llewelyn/Llewellyn, use of name, 53
Llewelyn Davies – *See* Davies
Llewellyn, (Ernest) Hugh, 81, 84
Llewellyn, (Evan) Donald, 81
Llewellyn, Gwendoline Elizabeth ('Gwen'), 78, 81
Llewellyn, (James) Harold, 81
Llewellyn, James Robert, 17, 20 81, 83, 92
Llewellyn, Mabel Bessie (later Jones, later Hann) ('May'), 4, 5, 11 *et seq*, 85, 89, 92, 95
Llewellyn, (Miriam) Lottie, 81
Llewellyn, Wilfrid Henry, 81
Llewellyn, (William) Edgar, 81
Llewellyns, the, 88
Lloyd George, Lady, 60
Lob, 60
London, 4, 7, 18, 33, 37, 46, 47, 56, 57, 69, 72, 87, 89, 92
London & South-West Railway, 15, 20
Long & Slow Winding Railway, 20
Long John Silver, 67
Luath, 23, 49, 55, 58, 99
Lucas, Audrey, 45, 62
Lucas, E(dward) V(errall), 45, 62, 80, 95
Lucas, (Florence) Elizabeth, 45, 62
Lusitania, S. S., 34

Manchester Guardian, 73
Marriott Watson, H(enry) B(rereton), 45
Marsden, Edward, 47
Mason, A(lfred) E(dward) W(oodley), 45, 46
Mason, Ellen E., 96

Mason, Ernold A., 96
Maurier, George
  See Du Maurier, George, 54
'May' – *See* Llewellyn, Mabel
Mayflower, 20, 69, 81, 83
Medstead, 15, 21, 68, 69, 77, 78, 80, 81, 83, 92, 95
Medstead railway station, 21, 70, 79
Meredith, George, 11, 34, 46, 61, 65
Meredith, Will, 46
Meyrick-Jones, Frederic, 47
Milborne St Andrew, 79
Millarship, Archibald, 43, 92
Milne, A(lan) A(lexander), 45
My Man Jeeves (Wodehouse), 48

Nana, 56
National Observer, 67
Nether Compton, 6
Neverland, 8
Newfoundland, 17
Newport, Christopher, 94
Nottingham Journal, 6
Nyren, John, 80

Ogilvy, Margaret (later Barrie), 6, 61
Old Harry, 11
Orcxy, Baroness Emmuska, 60
Ossian, 56
'Over the Alps', 75
Oxford, 63

Paddington, 36, 96
Page, Mrs, 52
Pankhursts, the, 55
Parsons, Mary, 77
Partridge, Bernard, 46
Pawling, Sydney, 47

Peter and Wendy (Barrie), 66
Peter Pan (Barrie), 7, 8, 29, 47, 53, 56, 59, 62, 66, 75, 78, 89, 94
Pfrangley, Charles ('Charlie'), 71
Pilkington, 94
Poole, 5, 11, 16, 17, 20, 71, 73, 81, 84
Poole Foundry, 84
Poole Harbour, 11, 84
Poole Pottery, 84
Poole School of Art and Technology, 84
Poole railway station, 20
Porthos, 23, 60
Portmadog, 16
Prisoner of Zenda, The (Hope), 46
Privateers, The (Marriott Watson), 46
Punch, 45, 46
Purdie, Mabel, 60

Quality Street (Barrie), 20

Raczkiewicz, Wladyslaw, 60
Rae, Christine, 72
Ranjitsinjhi, Prince, 45
Red Hill, Farnham, 22
Reddy, 66
Rooks Begin to Build, The (Barrie), 33
Ropley, 77
Rosalind (Barrie), 52, 98
Royal Hotel, Winchester, 15
Rupert and Mary (Barrie), 85
Rustington, 82
Ruthless Rhymes (Graham), 46

Salonika, 6
Salvation Army, 6, 15, 16
Samoa, 67
Sandbanks, 79
Sandford, 63
Scarlet Pimpernel, The (Orcxy), 60
Scott, Peter, 35, 60
Scott, Robert Falcon, 35, 92
Seaman, Owen, 45
Selborne, 72, 80, 95
Sentimental Tommy (Barrie), 66, 74
Shackleford, 40
Shand, Mitchell, 42
Silverdale, 46, 94
Sloane Square underground station, 68
Smith, Charles Turley, 45
Snook, Bessie (later Llewellyn), 17, 20, 78, 81
Snook, Ellinor, 14, 16
Snook, Emmanuel, 14, 17, 38
Snooks, the, 79
Southampton, 16, 17, 69
South-West Wind in the Woodland (Meredith), 34, 65
Spring, Anna, 63
St Andrews University, 7
St James's Gazette, 7, 33
St Pancras railway station, 33
Steam car, 43, 97
Steam Tactics (Kipling), 44
Stevenson, Robert Louis, 67
Surrey County Council, 44
Sutton, 16
Swinstead, George Hillyard, 47

Tennyson, Charles, 46
Terriss, Ellaline, 20
Terry, Ellen, 60
Tess of the D'Urbervilles (Hardy), 38
Thames (river), 63
Thomas, Elizabeth, 83

Thomas, Gwendolen, 6, 7, 83
Thomas, William, 6, 83
Tilford, 13, 23, 41, 53, 65, 68, 69, 78
Tilford Road, 13, 22, 43, 69
Tinkerbell, 75
Tomson, Graham R. – *See* Rosamund Ball
Tolpuddle Martyrs, 17
'Topsy' – *See* Jones, Marian
Treasure Island (Stevenson), 67
Trevelyan, Hilda, 53
Twa Dogs, The (Burns), 56

'Uncle Jim' – *See* Barrie, James Matthew

Vaudeville Theatre, 20
Vaughan, Brigadier-General, 6
Watercress Line, 69
Waterloo railway station, 75
Watson, George Spencer, 47
Waverley Abbey, 13, 22, 86
Waverley Abbey House, 13, 22, 85
Waverley Arms, 22
Waverley Estate, 13, 24, 65, 86
Waverley Mill, 13
Webb, Eliza, 63
Wells, H(erbert) G(eorge), 4
Wendy, 66
Wendy house, 66
Wendy's house, 29
Wessex Poems (Hardy), 38

Wesleyan Church, 17
West End (London), 32, 34, 53, 60
Wey (river), 13, 69
What Every Woman Knows (Barrie), 53, 61
What it is Coming To (Barrie), 85
Wilde, Oscar, 52
Winchester, 15, 23, 69, 75
Winchester railway station, 19, 21
Winter, Revd James, 72
Winter, Margaret ('Maggie') *See* Barrie, Margaret
Winter, William Henderson, 5, 15, 21, 25, 70, 72
Winter, William ('Willie'), 71, 73
Winters, the, 21, 68, 71, 77, 78, 81, 83, 88
Winterborne Whitechurch, 15, 17, 83
Wodehouse, P(elham) G(renville), 48
Women's Co-operative Guild, 55
Woods of Westermain, The (Meredith), 61
Wrexham, 5, 83, 92, 97
Wright, Orville, 68
Wright, Wilbur, 68
Wylie, David, 61
Wylie, James, 61
Wylie, Maggie, 61

Young Cricketer's Tutor, The (Nyren), 80